# MONITORS

## THE MEN, MACHINES AND MYSTIQUE

*To Terry Sweeney*

*I hope you enjoy this*

*Best Regards*

*Jerry*

## by Jerry L. Harlowe

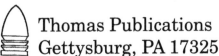
Thomas Publications
Gettysburg, PA 17325

*Them new-fangled iron ships ain't fit for hogs to go to sea in, let alone honest sailors!*

*You'll all go to the bottom in her, youngster, that's where you'll all go.*

*In memory*
*of all the men who did*
*go to the bottom in*
*"them new-fangled iron ships."*

# CONTENTS

Preface ...................................................................6

Monitor Classes of the Civil War Navy ....................8

Building the Machine .......................................14

A Few Good Men ............................................24

War Stories ..................................................46

Photo Gallery ...............................................70

Epilogue & More ............................................91

Endnotes ...................................................100

References Cited or Consulted .............................103

Index........................................................108

# PREFACE

The United States Navy came out of the Civil War as a force radically changed by the introduction, construction and successful employment of armored warships. With the collapse of the Southern Confederacy, the U.S. Navy as an institution found it difficult if not impossible to deal with the drastic changes wrought by a wartime leap in technology. April 1865 witnessed the end of General Lee's army and the beginning of the Confederacy's march into history. Much of the credit for the Southern defeat was owed to the Navy; however, most if not all of the credibility went to Grant's bloated Army of the Potomac. Accolades or not, the Union navy of 1865 was a force unequalled and unmatched by any navy in the world. From a sailing and steaming force of forty-two ships of various descriptions in April 1861, the national will and treasury created a navy of no less than 211 new ships. Among those ships, some sixty-eight were ironclads of various descriptions including nine monitor classes accounting for at least fifty-six of the iron warships. These new ships of wood and iron were bolstered and supplemented by other numerous ships which were purchased, seized, or captured and brought into war service. However, no matter the size and power of the immediate post Civil War navy, its might and glory would be brief.

In the American Civil War, the monitor class warships were no different in effect than their ancient revolutionary warship predecessors in such notable navies as Elizabethan England, Imperial Rome, the Greek city states or the early Neolithic marsh dwellers of northern Europe. The monitors were pure and simple expressions of the national government of the United States, instruments of political will to help assure that the nation would remain whole and not be rendered asunder by the cancer of slavery. The monitors were produced by a nation just a few years into the industrial revolution, conceptualized and designed by a Swedish immigrant, financed through new national taxation of the people and rushed to completion, with various degrees of success and utter failures. To meet the instant and unique naval needs presented by the fratricidal war the monitor class ironclad was plain, direct and so utterly commanding that they approached omnipresence in their operational element. The monitor class ships assisted the national government under the minority Republican president, Abraham Lincoln, to not only win the war and preserve the Union of the states, but to change the entire fabric of American political life and society. This set the stage for amending the Constitution with bold, radical changes in 1865, 1868, and the last in the three postwar amendments, 1870. Those amendments helped to guide the transformation of America into its second period of identity with renewed purpose.

This book is a series of vignettes addressing the unique and particularly odd, but singularly powerful ironclad warship classes designated as "monitors." It will not try to describe the decisions and minute details that went into the construction and utilization of these machines, if in fact that could be accomplished. It is but a brief introduction which will highlight some of the ships, a few of the special and not so special men involved with the vessels, and touch on the "mystique" that developed around these floating flatirons which was unlike that of any other class of American warship.

Undoubtedly, the initial design and construction of the monitor class was revolutionary in concept and execution. Commander Charles Davis, a member of the first ironclad board, made some interesting remarks concerning the plans presented for the first monitor. One Mr. C. S. Bushnell, a naval constructor from New York, presented the Ericsson plan and model to Commander Davis and the Board. Presuming Mr. Bushnell and his presented plan to be the work of cranks, Commander Davis told Mr. Bushnell very directly:

> *...take this little thing home with you and worship it, as it would not be idolatry, because it was in the image of nothing in the heaven above or on the earth beneath or in the waters under the earth.*

This was quite a comment, on a ship design that would be no less than a revolution, save the Union navy and dominate the international naval power. The monitor design was, in fact, unlike anything before on the seas, large iron plated leaps in technology and purpose.

> *...for the indigenous American capital ship concept, the monitor, resistance to experiment meant an end evolution. We had the perfect ship to defend America's coasts and harbors. The monitor was a design whose exact lines had become equated to the symbol and its function. To change or to enlarge it might mean a corollary expansion in the mission itself. And it was, moreover, a design that seemed forever "modern."[1]*

However, the monitor concept did grow in size, technology, and purpose in such a linear development that it is considered a direct descendant of the ultimate expression of the naval gun platform, the IOWA class battleships of World War II.

Today, the monitors are all gone. Only a quiet mystique lives on, composed from handed down antique stories, refined by generations of storytellers, and continued by scholarship and amateur research. This amalgam of fanciful fabrication and the truth is, in reality, the monitor story.

# Monitor Classes

## of the

# Civil War Navy

For more complete information on the specifications of any of the monitors, it is best to consult the *Official Records of the Union and Confederate Navies in the War of the Rebellion*, Series II, Vol. I. Most published data on the monitors find their genesis in this worthy reference set produced by the United States Government under an Act of Congress, 1894. The entire work is still available in the original printing and in a faithfully reprinted version.

Another fine reference is Donald Canney's *The Old Steam Navy, The Ironclads, 1842-1885*. Anyone even remotely interested in American ironclad warships, as well as the monitors, will find this book "must reading" on the subject.

The information on the following pages serves as an introduction to the ships and the classes under which they were produced. These were wonderful ships of evolution and revolution, and as such contained hundreds of new patents covering manifold inventions from construction techniques to flushing marine heads.

## Monitor: 1 Ship

Brainchild of the singularly focused and irascible genius, John Ericsson, the construction of this steam powered, turreted ship was a fundamental departure from all contemporary naval architecture. The ship demonstrated her significance, untested and under fire, within a few, short hours in battle with the Rebel ironclad C.S.S. *Virginia* at Hampton Roads, Virginia. *Monitor's* success forever changed the face of naval warfare.

| Ship Name: | U.S.S. *Monitor* |
| --- | --- |
| Contractor: | John Ericsson |
| Overall length: | 172' |
| Extreme beam: | 41' 6" |
| Draft: | 10' 6" |
| Designed speed: | 9 knots |
| Armament: | Two 15-inch Dahlgren smoothbores |

## Passaic: 10 Ships

The Passaic class was essentially an enlarged Monitor, built in the same basic fashion, but with some improvements over the original ship. The turret armor was increased from 8 to 11 inches, gun specifications called for two 15-inch Dahlgren smoothbores, ventilation was improved, a permanent, armored smokestack was installed and the pilot house was relocated from the bow to a position atop the turret where it would not block the field of fire. As a class, these ships saw the most combat with Confederate forces and proved to be worthy far beyond their average contract price of about $400,000 each.

Ship Names: U.S.S. *Camanche, Catskill, Lehigh, Montauk, Nahant, Nantucket, Passaic, Patapsco, Sangamon, Weehawken.*

| Overall length: | 200' |
| Extreme beam: | 46' |
| Draft: | 10' 6" |
| Designed speed: | 7 knots |
| Designed armament: | 2 15-inch Dahlgren smoothbores |
| Actual armament: | |
| *Camanche:* | 2 15-inch smoothbores |
| *Lehigh* & | |
| *Patapsco:* | 1 15-inch Dahlgren smoothbore and 1 150-pdr. Parrott rifle. |

The remainder all had one 11-inch and one 15-inch Dahlgren smoothbore.

# Canonicus:  9 Ships

Although outwardly similar in appearance to the Passaics, these nine ships were the first to incorporate the experience of combat. The failures, successes, and battle endurance of the original Monitor and of the following monitors of the Passaic class were recorded and studied, giving birth to a large number of improvements to be incorporated into these still larger vessels.

However, the design changes ordered by the Navy, as the ships were being built, were constant and seriously interrupted the construction schedules. Many of the changes required serious effort on the part of the builders and became so involved as to lead to a series of lawsuits against the Federal government. The contractors absorbed much in the way of cost overruns. The court actions they instituted to recover their losses continued literally for decades subsequent to the war. Again, efforts to improve armor, turret protection, updated ventilation and the final armament of the ships with 2 15-inch guns led to a formidable ship of war.

It should be noted that this class of ship is the only class of monitor that survives intact to this day. Beyond the capsized and depth-charged shattered remains of U.S.S. *Monitor* lying in perilous waters off Cape Hatteras, N.C., the U.S.S. *Tecumseh* rests upside down in the muddy bottom of Mobile Bay, Alabama. She has been entombed in the muck of the bay and today this ship is a unique time capsule to August 5, 1864, the day she went to the bottom.

Sadly, our nation has not found *Tecumseh* worthy of expending the national treasury to recover and preserve this one-of-a-kind American naval relic. As a nation we could learn a serious lesson from the British who have expended considerable time and money to preserve a vestige of their naval heritage.

Ship Names:  U.S.S. *Canonicus, Catawba, Mahopac, Manayunk, Manhattan, Oneota, Saugus, Tecumseh, Tippecanoe.*

Note: The ships varied slightly, as completed, due to the changes incorporated in the individual ships as they were being built.

| Overall length: | 225' |
| Extreme beam: | 43' |
| Draft: | 11' 6" |
| Designed speed: | 13 knots |
| Armament: | 2 15-inch Dahlgren smoothbores |

# Yazoo (Casco):  20 Ships

The purpose of the design was to provide the navy with a "light draft" monitor, capable of navigating the shallow Southern rivers and back bays and delivering a 15-inch punch to any Rebel ironclad or fortification willing to contest the ship's passage.

Although the concept was Ericsson's, he begged off the project as he was fully engaged with the construction and design of several other monitors at the time. The design and construction of these ships were turned over to Alban Stimers, an egotistical, but politically well-connected naval officer who, in the end, suffered little for the disservice he performed for the United States Navy. He proved to be the wrong man for the job, woefully unequal to the task before him.

Without a doubt, this class of monitor represented the greatest waste of money, time, shipbuilding talent and national resources ever spent in the United States up to that time. None of these ships saw active service against Confederate forces in their true monitor form. Fifteen of the ships were launched after the war was over, essentially scrap for sale.

Ship Names:  U.S.S. *Casco, Chimo, Cohoes, Etlah, Klamath, Koka, Modoc, Napa, Naubuc, Nausett, Shawnee, Shiloh, Squando, Suncook, Tunxis, Umpqua, Wassuc, Waxsaw, Yazoo, Yuma.*

| | |
|---|---|
| Overall Length: | 225' |
| Extreme beam: | 45' |
| Designed draft: | 6' |
| Speed: | 9 knots |
| Armament: | |

# Miantonomoh:  4 Ships

Perhaps the best ships of the monitor class to be built and launched, only one was completed in time to take an active part in the closing months of the war.  All of the vessels were constructed in government navy yards and reflected well on the quality of work that the yards were capable of putting out on such experiential vessels.

Following the close of the war, two ships of this class made extended oceanic voyages proving that these ships were indeed capable of meeting, on the high seas, the best ships the rest of the world had to offer.  The U.S.S. *Monadnock* sailed to San Francisco via Cape Horn and U.S.S. *Miantonomoh* sailed the North Atlantic to show the flag in European waters.  On his way to California, the captain of the *Monadnock*, John Rogers, had to consider carefully the possibility of starting a naval war with Spain. And while in Europe, the impressive *Miantonomoh* acted as a base for naval intelligence, as the calling card for the Assistant Secretary of the Navy Fox, and as a reminder to the Europeans that the monitor system was a valid naval weapon upon which the United States could carry its national will, if it so wished. *Miantonomoh's* cruise also set the stage for the treaty that would allow the United States to purchase the Alaska territories from the Russians in 1867.

All four ships were in short order laid up and dismantled. However, their hulks were exploited in the corrupt Naval Department during the Grant Administration; their old names were attached to new ships being built under the guise of repair to the Civil War vintage ships.

Ship Names:  U.S.S. *Agamenticus, Miantonomoh, Monadnock, Tonawanda.*

| | |
|---|---|
| Overall Length: | 258' 6" |
| Extreme Beam: | 52' 9" |
| Draft: | 12' 8" |
| Designed speed: | Unknown, recorded service speeds 6 1/2 to 9 knots |
| Armament: | 4 15-inch Dahlgren smoothbores |

# Kalamazoo:  4 Ships

These monitors were designed to be the crowning glory of the Monitor concept.  They were the largest and most expensive ships of the monitor class ever ordered.  However, as the war raced along to its predictable end, the construction of these war ships slowed and eventually halted, incomplete.  These grand machines rotted on the building ways and eventually were broken-up as so much kindling wood.

Ship Names: U.S.S. *Kalamazoo,
Passaconaway, Quinsigamond,
Shackamaxon.*

| | |
|---|---|
| Overall length: | 345' |
| Extreme beam: | 56' 8" |
| Draft: | 17' 6" |
| Designed speed: | 10 knots |
| Armament: | 4 15-inch Dahlgren smoothbores |

# Roanoke: 1 Ship

Although not designed as a monitor, U.S.S. *Roanoke* was classified as such after her rebuilding. Originally she was a steam frigate in the same class as U.S.S. *Merrimac*, another ship that went through a more radical and well known conversion into the Confederate ironclad, C.S.S. *Virginia*.

*Roanoke's* full ship's hull was cut down to provide a low freeboard, her deck and sides plated. Plans were made to install four gun turrets of the Ericsson type. However, the ship was not strong enough to support the weight of four turrets called for in the initial specifications. The turrets were decreased by one, but even with three turrets the ship was unable to provide a platform that was stable at sea. *Roanoke's* center of gravity was much higher than the designed monitors, and with the tremendous weight of the gun turrets she rolled heavily at sea. For the most part, this experiment in monitor conversion was a qualified failure, but the ship did engage in some shore bombardment late in the war. However, for the most part, *Roanoke* spent her active career as a station or guard ship and was thereafter restrained to harbor duty. The *U.S.S. Roanoke,* somewhat the Frankenstein's monster of monitors, was sold in 1883 and broken-up.

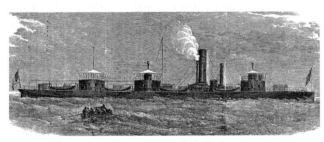

| | |
|---|---|
| Ship Name: | U.S.S. *Roanoke* |
| Overall length: | 265' |
| Extreme Beam: | 52' 6" |
| Draft: | 24' 3" |

| | |
|---|---|
| Designed speed: | 10 knots |
| Armament: | 3 15-inch Dahlgren smoothbores (one per turret), 2 150-pdr. Parrott rifles (fore & aft turret), 1 11-inch Dahlgren smoothbore (center turret). |

# Dictator: 1 Ship

Designed by and constructed under the supervision of John Ericsson, this ship was to be his personal expression of the ultimate monitor, a true seagoing ship. When sent down the launching ways, *Dictator's* overall length was second to none of the monitors completed, but she proved to be an utter failure. With Ericsson's authority cemented by his larger-than-life fame, *Dictator* was brought into commission by the naval hero Captain John Rodgers. This consummate naval officer suffered the big ship's shortcomings but, "...though convinced Ericsson was a genius, [Rodgers] also termed him an obstinate fool."[1] *Dictator* failed to ever come close to obtaining or living up to the standards of her concept, design, and construction, and although much was expected of the ship, *Dictator* never tasted battle.

| | |
|---|---|
| Ship Name: | U.S.S. *Dictator* |
| Overall length: | 312' |
| Extreme beam: | 50' |
| Draft: | 20' 6" |
| Designed speed: | 15 knots |
| Armament: | 2 15-inch smoothbores |

# Puritan: 1 Ship

Somewhat of a larger, almost sister ship to the U.S.S. *Dictator*, she too was designed and contracted for construction to John Ericsson. The Navy Department wanted this ship to have two turrets, but the know-it-all inventor wanted another enormous monitor, single turret, carrying two 20-inch smoothbores. The navy at first prevailed, but relented to a single turret concept after the hull of the ship had been in the water for over a year. With the end of the war, construction delays and failures with the casting of the new 20-inch smoothbores, completion of the ship was doomed. The hull languished until the 1876 near-war with Spain, when the U.S. Congress opened the purse of the national treasury to continue construction. But the vessel completed under the name of the Civil War designed monitor was vastly different from the concepts and technologies available to John Ericsson.

| Ship Name: | U.S.S. *Puritan* |
| --- | --- |
| Overall Length: | 340' |
| Extreme beam: | 50' |
| Draft: | 20' |
| Designed speed: | 15 knots |
| Armament: | 2 20-inch smoothbores |

# Onondaga: 1 Ship

A much photographed and fine ship, U.S.S. *Onondaga* served her entire war career on the James River. She was the first double-turreted monitor commissioned. Although assigned to a somewhat less glamorous role in the James River, *Onondaga's* service and very presence was critical to the ultimate success of the Army of the Potomac as it pounded General Lee's ragtag, but lethal, Army of Northern Virginia into submission.

The *Onondaga* returned from the war without damage and was sold back to her builder, under a special law provided by Congress, for the same amount as her contract price. This sweetheart deal also allowed the contractor to resell the ship into the French Navy. In service to the French, *Onondaga* retained her name, was modified somewhat to suit the French, and over the years remained in naval service as a coastal defense ship until 1903.

| Ship Name: | U.S.S. *Onondaga* |
| --- | --- |
| Overall length: | 226' |
| Extreme Beam: | 49' 3" |
| Draft: | 12' 10" |
| Designed speed: | 9 knots |
| Armament: | 2 15-inch smoothbores |
| | 2 150-pdr. Parrott rifle |

# The River Monitors

During the war, there were more naval actions of consequence on the Mississippi and other Western Theater rivers than any other theater of naval battle. The vessels designed, built and converted for both Union and Confederate naval service were different, quite a study and story in and of themselves. Among the vessels were four monitor classes designed especially for operations in the shallow interior waterways of the country, facing the unique style of naval warfare imposed by the geography of the rivers and the land through which they coursed their way to the seas. These monitors were too weak in their hulls to ever venture out into the high seas and therefore did not pose a threat to any of the European powers. They were a breed apart, adapted by naval evolution to their particular environment.

Along with their own breed of monitor, the Western designers came up with an improved version of the turret which operated mainly with steam. An innovative redesign, it was never fully appreciated by the Navy Department, due to the seemingly impenetrable "cult of Ericsson" that existed in the Department and held sway over many decisions.

James Eads, a prolific designer and builder, went Ericsson one better in turret design but was not allowed to place his turret on a ship unless it was matched on that ship with a turret of Ericsson's design. Several monitors were built under this strange arrangement and two of them, U.S.S. *Chickasaw* and U.S.S. *Winnebago*, participated in Admiral Farragut's attack on the forts guarding the entrance to Mobile Bay and the Confederate naval forces waiting to contest their passage within the bay. It was the large guns on these two ships that forced the issue of the surrender of C.S.S. *Tennessee*. The new turret was a match, if not somewhat better than the Ericsson design.

The river monitors were designed differently and for the special environment of riverine warfare, and most importantly, not designed by Ericsson. I've elected not to include images of the river monitors in this work so as not to confuse the issue of design and purpose. Again, consultation of other works on these monitors will give the reader a further insight into the war on the rivers and its special considerations.

# Neosho:  2 Ships

These ironclads were the first monitors designed by noted Mississippi River builder, James B. Eads. They were a breed apart and known for their shallow draft of less than five feet. Their machinery, contained in a humpback deck, propelled the ship through a stern paddle wheel contained within an armored paddle-box. Of light construction, the ships were incapable of deep water operations but worked remarkably well in the service on the western rivers.

 Ship Names:  U.S.S. *Neosho, Osage*
 Overall length:  180'
 Extreme beam:  45'
 Draft:  4' 6"
 Service speed:  7.5 knots
 Armament:  2 11-inch smoothbores

# Ozark:  1 Ship

This ship was a ungainly mix of traditional Mississippi River steamboat design with a turret added. She was built with a large deckhouse to provide crew quarters above decks, and carried a 10-inch and two 9-inch guns in unprotected deck mounts, in addition to the two 11-inch guns mounted in the turret. Although an impressive artillery platform, she was ponderous and slow and overall, not a desirable machine of war. A naval engineer remarked of the Ozark, "a fleet of such vessels would ruin the nation."[2]

 Ship Name:  U.S.S. *Ozark*
 Overall length:  180'
 Extreme beam:  50'
 Draft:  5'
 Service speed:  2.5 knots
 Armament:  2 11-inch smoothbores (in turret); 2 9-inch smoothbores (open mount); 1 10-inch smoothbore (open mount).

# Marietta:  2 Ships

These two ships were designed by the contractors and suffered changes insisted upon by the naval inspectors while they were being built. They were laid down in the summer of 1862, but not accepted into the navy until April 1866! Needless to say, these ships were extremely slow in building. Another quirk regarding these two ships is that no one knows for sure what they looked like upon completion. There are no known pictorial representations of the vessels as they were completed. Maybe in someone's attic out there....

 Ship Names:  U.S.S. *Marietta, Sandusky*.
 Overall length:  170'
 Extreme beam:  50'
 Draft:  5'
 Designed speed:  9 knots
 Armament:  2 11-inch smoothbores

# Milwaukee:  4 Ships

James B. Eads designed and built these four ships that were without equal on the rivers. Although of light draft and designed for shallow water operations, they spent some active service with the West Gulf Blockading Squadron, notably with Admiral Farragut's fleet at Mobile Bay. The point blank fire delivered by U.S.S. *Winnebago* and U.S.S. *Chickasaw* helped to knock out the Rebel ironclad C.S.S. *Tennessee* and disperse the remaining Rebel ships.

 Ship Names:  U.S.S. *Chickasaw, Kickapoo, Milwaukee, Winnebago*.
 Overall length:  229'
 Extreme Beam:  56'
 Draft:  6'
 Designed speed:  9 knots
 Armament:  4 11-inch smoothbores

# BUILDING THE MACHINE

## John Ericsson

...he has valuable ideas-and the government should have them—The world is indebted to him for the screw propellor [sic], for the monitors, for the hot air engine, and in large part, for the monster ordnance—He is a genius; and an obstinate fool—He sees what other men do not, and cannot see plain things—He is a genius to be used, not a man of sense to be followed—and yet so cranky and opinionated that [any] doubt at his conclusions is an insult, or a proof of enmity, or gross stupidity of a thought—[1]

*John Ericsson*
*The genius behind the monitors.*

## Gideon Wells

Writing in his diary after receiving word about the loss of U.S.S. *Monitor* at sea, Gideon Wells reflected:

*She (Monitor) is a primary representative of a class identified with my administration of the Navy. Her novel construction and qualities I adopted and she was built amidst obloquy and ridicule. Such a change in the character of a fighting vessel few naval men, or any Secretary under their influence, would have taken the responsibility of adopting.[2]*

Gideon Wells was appointed by President Lincoln as Secretary of the Navy in March 1861. A somewhat vain man, the 59 year old Mr. Wells wore a flowing wig which had the effect of highlighting his undeniable whiskers and accentuating the energy of this Connecticut newspaper editor. His talent in organization had served the Navy Department well when he served as chief of the Bureau of Provisions and Clothing during the earlier war with Mexico. But, when Wells left the Democratic Party to join the Republican Party in 1855 it created the right circumstances for his subsequent appointment by Lincoln. The president needed a good mix of politics and geographic rationality in making his political selections, and Gideon Wells filled the bill. Regardless of the reason for his selection, Wells proved to be a stroke of pure genius—the prover-

# The Ironclad Board, 1861

*Gideon Wells*
*Secretary of the Navy.*

bial *right man at the right time*. His energy and direction remolded the Navy Department and provided him the distinction of serving in that capacity during the Lincoln and Andrew Johnson administrations.

As an early and true believer in the ironclad, Wells is almost singular within the government in his support and promotion of the monitor concept. The Secretary was quick to recognize and reward the men who fought his ironclads, but he is equally hard on those who dared to be critical or fail. Wells saw to the sacking of Admiral DuPont after the unfortunate Admiral failed to take Charleston, South Carolina with an ironclad fleet boasting 7 of the newest Passaic class monitors and 2 additional ironclad warships. Although the adventure was destined for failure, Wells did not see it that way and decided to replace the Admiral with someone who would do the job right. The Secretary may have been the first priest in the cult of the monitor, for his faith in the ironclads was strong.

In the end, Gideon Wells was nonetheless an engaging and first rate administrator. He had an extraordinarily practical vision when it came to supporting and promoting the monitors and the men who fought them, and, he served his presidents well.

With the news of the Rebels building an ironclad from the remains of U.S.S. *Merrimac*, Congress decided it was past time to start looking for a ship to meet the monster ship as she steamed her way up the Potomac River to deliver some messages from the Confederate States in the form of iron shot and shell. Her transformation from destroyed U.S. property to Confederate Navy ironclad was accompanied with a name change to C.S.S. *Virginia*. Daily reports flooded the capital on the fearsome ship and its destructive powers to such an extent that the U.S. Congress was, in fact, just short of panic.

The first action by Congress was to appoint a board to investigate the possibilities of completing the Stevens' steam battery as an answer to C.S.S. *Virginia's* threat. The steam battery had languished for years on the builders' stocks for lack of real need to complete the ship. The board's report was not made until the end of 1861, but by then other answers were in the works.

An extra session of Congress was declared by the new president that summer and on the third day of August the U.S. Congress passed legislation to provide the money and direction for the construction of armored ships and floating batteries for the Navy. The law called for an examining board of three seasoned naval officers to review the proposals and specification to be submitted in response to the Navy's printed public notice for such ships. Four days later the Navy Department issued advertisements for ironclad ships and brief specifications for their size and service. On the eighth day of August, the Board was selected. The final three to serve were Commodore Joseph Smith, Commodore Hiram Paulding and Commander Charles Davis. Three of the most unlikely individuals that could be imagined to serve as officers responsible for the selection of ships that were radical in concept from any ship that any one of them ever delt with in a long career of naval service.

The officers set to the task and by September 16, submitted their report which covered the plans and proposals for at least seventeen ships. Of the three ships recommended for building,

*Commodore Joseph Smith, Commodore Hiram Paulding and Commander Charles Davis.*

the most radical was the *Monitor*. Although convinced to accept John Ericsson's design, the board put a severe restriction on her building and service by stating that her acceptance was conditional, "...with a guarantee and forfeiture in case of failure in any of the properties and points of the vessel as proposed."[3] If *Monitor* failed to be an unqualified success, she would not be paid for by the government.

It was difficult for the ancient officers to select *Monitor* as one of their three choices. At one point in the process, Commander Charles Davis belittled Ericsson's plan by telling Charles Bushnell, who was presenting the plans on behalf of John Ericsson:

> *Take this little thing home with you and worship it, as it would not be idolatry, because it was in the image of nothing in the heaven above or on the earth beneath or in the waters under the earth.[4]*

However, as a board, they were able to deal with their prejudices and shortcomings. In their report to Congress, they honestly stated the problem by writing:

> *Distrustful of our ability to discharge this duty, which the law requires should be performed by three skillful naval officers, we approach the subject with diffidence, having no experience and but scanty knowledge in this branch of naval architecture.[5]*

From this board came three ironclads: *Galena*, *New Ironsides*, and *Monitor*. *Galena* would prove a miserable failure as an ironclad, be stripped of her plating and serve the remainder of the war as a wooden steamer. The U.S.S. *New Ironsides* would serve throughout the war and provide a stable platform for intense bombardment provided by her broadside gun arrangement. Shortly after the war she would be destroyed by fire. The U.S.S. *Monitor* saved the day and the Federal fleet at Hampton Roads, Virginia just a short six months later. Her fame was insured and her memory made immortal with her loss in December 1862 during a gale off the North Carolina capes. All in all, the old salty board did a fine job.

# Abraham Lincoln

*"All I have to say is what the girl said when she stuck her foot in the stocking. It strikes me there's something in it."[6]*

The back woods lawyer had done it again. On September 13, 1861, President Lincoln in the company of C.S. Bushnell made a personal visit to the ironclad board. Their trip was at the behest of the politically connected shipbuilder Bushell of New Haven, Connecticut, to present the plans and model of John Ericsson's floating battery for consideration. Bushnell had stumbled over the plans while conferring with Ericsson on the stability of another less radical

*Lincoln was a regular visitor to the Washington Navy Yard.
Note the Capitol dome above the boat house roof.*

ironclad that Bushnell had himself presented to the board for consideration. The Yankee ship-builder knew a good thing when he saw it, but his eye was on profits and building. Lincoln's eye was different. The presentation made on behalf of the ship did not impress the board sufficiently, even with *Monitor's* main detractor Commander Charles Davis absent, to accept this plan for a radical departure from conventional naval architecture. Later, Davis would not be sold at all on the idea until a direct appeal and presentation was made by none other then the brooding genius John Ericsson himself. However, on this day, President Lincoln's keen eye and powerful intuition led him to make the above observation with regard to the strange little ship presented to him for his support. This appreciation and innate military understanding of the novel warship, would spark the president's curiosity. He became a regular visitor to the naval yard as he had a deep appreciation and fascination with mechanical devices and new attractions and inventions always drew his interest.

With the president's full support, the ironclad board approved the construction of *Monitor*, along with two other ironclad ships that were much more conservative in their approach to the ironclad question. *Monitor's* delivery had been promised within 100 days of contract, and it was delivered on time. Lincoln's vision and lobbying was well awarded as the unconventional ironclad fought an epic and now classic duel with C.S.S. *Virginia* and changed the face of naval warfare. Although there was abundant chest-beating by the Union forces after the battle, only one person, Lincoln, truly realized the value of *Monitor*. Somewhere in the flood of telegrams following the engagement, Gideon Wells, Secretary of the Navy, passed on the immediate concerns of the president to Gustavus Fox, Assistant Secretary of the Navy at Fort Monroe:

> *The President directs that the* Monitor *be not too much exposed...*[7]

Fox, who had telegraphed Wells earlier that Monitor was ready at the instant to reengage the Rebel ram was most likely distressed with the President's caution.

However, the backwoods lawyer turned president knew that *Monitor's* true value in this dangerous situation was not another muzzle-to-muzzle shootout with the Rebel ship. *Monitor's* presence was all that was needed to neutralize *Virginia's* offensive capability. If the Rebels gambled and lost *Virginia*, there was no way to stop the Yankee ironclad from steaming to Norfolk or even up the James River to the Rebel capital of Richmond. Although the presence of *Virginia* did not allow General McClellan's army a supply base on the James River for his halting Peninsular Campaign, the Union Army was still in good shape and in no fear of having its communications and supplies cut with its supply base on the York River. If *Monitor* tried to destroy *Virginia* and in turn was destroyed or captured by the Rebel forces, the blockade would be raised and McClellan's army would be hard pressed to keep the field with its York River supply route threatened by *Virginia*. President Lincoln realized all this, and most importantly, acted in a timely and decisive manner to provide direction for the proper employment of *Monitor*. Although *Monitor's* iron sheathing and her two 11-inch guns could face anything the Confederates had to throw at her, Lincoln understood her value, and directed her employment as he saw fit. Writing after the war, *Virginia's* chief engineer spoke to Lincoln's policy of not endangering *Monitor* in another battle when it was not necessary to gain their objective of containing the Rebel ironclad. In part he wrote:

*When the* Merrimac *had steamed within two miles of the fort we plainly made out the* Monitor, *the iron battery Naugatuck, and other war vessels at anchor under Fort Monroe. The* Merrimac *steamed around in a large circle, which at one point brought her within one and one-half miles of her antagonist offering battle in deep water and upon their own ground— vain endeavor!*[8]

President Lincoln's support of the navy and its ironclads was unwavering throughout the war. He saw to its funding, and fully realized that the Civil War he was fighting would never be won without building a substantial force of ships. The U.S.S. *Monitor* may have been the invention of the genius Ericsson, but she was the Union's dream come true with the help of Lincoln's vision.

# Erastus Corning

Erastus Corning, a native New England Yankee, represents another aspect of building war machines such as the monitor class ships. Born in the last decade of the previous century, by the time of the Civil War Corning was a very successful self-made man, of great wealth, status and political influence.

As a youth Corning had been apprenticed into his uncle's hardware business in Troy, New York. He learned his lessons well and by age 20 formed a partnership in the hardware business after his move to Albany. Based on his hard

*Erastus Corning*

work and resulting profits, by age 32, Corning was settled and financed enough to purchase a small foundry and rolling mill specializing in nail production. As his iron business expanded he brought in a partner. The successful iron works and Corning's respectable business and political sense acted as a natural conduit into other business ventures. Corning became president of the New York Central Railroad for twelve years, and served later as mayor of the city of Albany. Additionally, he served in the New York State Senate and in Congress for several terms.

With his move into fulltime politics, Corning became a silent partner in his own iron works. As a member of the U.S. Congress, he was prohibited from receiving government contracts. But his Albany Iron Works received a hefty contract for the production of iron plate for the new navy ship-of-war, U.S.S. *Monitor*. The steam powered Albany Iron Works covered an area of over 40 acres, and with the new war and its production capability, the iron works was in an excellent position to help meet an urgent need, and profit handsomely.

It took all manner of men to build *Monitor*; some dreamed, some labored, and some fashioned iron plates..., but no matter the skill, it required money and power to get the project going, and those men who had invested their power base and personal wealth, such as Corning, enjoyed the fruits of their investments. As always, no matter how noble the cause, there was money to be made in war, and money was no problem for a government at war. Erastus Corning was but one man in an army of Yankee entrepreneurs who, with the help of the national treasury firing the furnaces of their business, helped to fashion a wartime navy replete with ironclad monitors.

# Porter's Assessment

In the early months of the war, Commander David D. Porter was assigned to inspect the new Ericsson battery that was under construction in New York and, "...to make a critical examination of the vessel and report my opinion of her capabilities."[9] There was abundant ridicule of Ericsson's so called "iron pot" in the newspapers, within the Navy Department, and in public and private debate. So great was the apprehension about John Ericsson's little ship that the contract awarded to the brooding and irritable in-

*Rear Admiral David D. Porter*

ventor was deliberately drafted in such a way that the ship was not to be fully paid for by the government until *Monitor* proved her worth in battle. Universal ill will surrounded the ship and its inventor as pressure increased to get it built, fitted out and on its way south to meet the Rebel ship being built in Norfolk, Virginia. Into this caldron stepped Porter.

Commander Porter met with the strange genius in New York, and the inventor took a prompt dislike to the navy man. John Ericsson was aghast that Porter, with no practical experience in shipbuilding mathematics or construction, would be the person the Navy Department sent to pass judgement! Keeping his gentleman's demeanor and even temperament, David D. Porter inspected the iron ship on her building ways. Carefully inspecting this and that and always taking notice, Porter was followed step for step by Ericsson. The inventor hounded Commander Porter with insults that Ericsson thought justified by his superior intellect, allowing him to heap abuse upon the unworthy naval officer. Although not in the same mental league as the irritable Swede, Commander Porter was nonetheless impressed by what he observed. He immediately related his approval of the vessel to the fussing Ericsson—in glowing terms. The astonished inventor had a hard time believing his ears. He had an even harder time thanking Porter for an unbiased opinion. Commander Porter later wrote:

> *Ericsson regarded me in astonishment, then seized my hand and almost shook my arm off. "My God!" he exclaimed, "and all this time I took you for a d——d fool, and you are not a d——d fool after all"*[10]

Although hounded and endlessly insulted by the "genius" Ericsson, Porter was ever the consummate professional. He remained objective enough in his duty to country and the naval service to inspect and form a positive opinion of *Monitor* as she was being brought to form.

After completion of the inspection, Commander Porter took his well earned leave from the now approving Ericsson and, "...telegraphed at once to the Navy Department, 'Mr. Ericsson's vessel is the best fighting machine ever invented, and can destroy any ship afloat.'"[11]

# U.S.S. Monitor What's in a Name?

New York, January 20, 1862

Sir.—In accordance with your request I now submit for your approbation a name for the floating battery at Greenpoint.

The impregnable and aggressive character of this structure will admonish the leaders of the Southern Rebellion that the batteries on the banks of their rivers will no longer present barriers to the entrance of the Union forces.

The ironclad intruder will thus prove a severe monitor to those leaders. But there are other leaders who will be startled and admonished by the booming of the guns from the impregnable iron turret. "Downing Street" will hardly view with indifference this last "Yankee notion," this monitor. To the Lords of the Admiralty the new craft will be a *monitor*, suggesting doubts as to the propriety of completing those four steel-clad ships at three and a half million apiece.

On these and many similar grounds I propose to name the new battery, *"Monitor."*

Your obedient servant,
J. Ericsson

To Gustavus V. Fox,
Assistant Secretary of the Navy[12]

# The 15-inch Dahlgren Smoothbore Shell Gun

Within the several classes of monitors, the armament mounted in the turrets included several types of large guns including the 11-inch Dahlgren smoothbore, the 150 pdr. Parrott rifle with 8-inch bore and the monster 15-inch Dahlgren smoothbore. Initially, the most predominant was the 11-inch Dahlgren smoothbore, which served well throughout the war. But with the introduction of the 15-inch gun, the U.S. Navy had a remarkable weapon. That singular weapon was the naval gun that secured the monitors, especially the large sea-going ships, as being above and beyond the best in the world, British and French fleets included.

John Dahlgren, architect of the gun system bearing his name, did not endorse the use of his design in the manufacture of the 15-inch gun, at least, not in the way the navy intended to manufacture the weapon. Dahlgren preferred the introduction and use of his 13-inch gun, for which the turrets of the new Passaic class monitors had been designed to accommodate. However, it was the 15-inch weapon that received the final approval from the navy. This was based, in part, on one very important proponent of the larger weapon, the assistant secretary of the navy:

*U.S.S.* Sangamon *on the James River, 1865.*

*Near the end of the war, a supply of 15-inch naval guns await shipment at the Brooklyn Navy Yard.*

*"...Assistant Secretary of the Navy Gustavus Fox [had] been impressed by the 15-inch Rodman at Ft. Monroe, [and he] pushed for similar sized guns for the turrets of the new monitors."[13]*

Dahlgren, soured by the Navy Department's endorsement and selection of the larger gun, withdrew any personal responsibility for the 15-inch weapon. His conclusion was that the larger guns were being rushed into manufacture and deployment and that haste did not set well with Dahlgren. The Navy Department would not receive his endorsement.

With or without Dahlgren's blessings and directions, 50 guns were scheduled by the Navy for production in the first contract of April 1862. A completion date of 120 days was called for. It was a task of heroic proportions; the guns weighed 21 tons and were to be mounted on iron carriages to carry their massive weight and power. Manufacture of the weapon was to be in the Rodman process and not the process that had previously been used on the Dahlgren gun. The Rodman process cut down construction time considerably and the navy's instant desire for the large guns necessitated a departure from the method employed in building the previous naval weapons.

As built, the range of the gun, using a 35 pound naval gunpowder load to discharge a 350 pound shell was 2100 yards, or just under 1 1/4 miles. Increasing the charge to 50 pounds resulted in only a gain of 300 yards in range at the maximum elevation of seven degrees. But the limited range was of little consequence since ship to ship warfare was still fought, up close and very personal. The need was not for range, but for destructive shock. Aiming the beast, at fighting ranges measured in several hundreds of yards, was essentially looking down the length of the barrel and pulling the lanyard when the enemy was in front of the cannon. At point blank ranges of 600 yards or less, the massive shot from the monster gun slammed into its victim in slightly more time than a human heartbeat. Its effect was staggering, destructive shock.

As the first 15-inch guns were mounted in the Passaic class monitors, they quickly became the odd duck within the turret. Since not enough of the guns had been produced to provide for two guns each for the delivery of the new monitors, the large gun was mounted next to an 11-inch gun. Additionally, the gun ports on the new monitors had been designed and constructed for the smaller proposed 13-inch gun. Therefore the muzzle of the 15-inch gun did not even fit through the turret's gun port. Consequently, a smoke box was designed and fitted to the muzzle to protect the gun crew from the blast of the gun when fired.

As odd as it seems, the gun was actually discharged within the turret, with the blast and ball finding their way out of the gun port piercing the thick iron turret. This dicey situation was not rectified until a later production of the 15-inch gun that lengthened the barrel, which was then turned-down to properly extend from the gun port. Also, the situation of the interior smoke box, or concussion box as it was also called, did not allow the gun captain to see his intended target.

As reported from U.S.S. *Passaic*, the 15-inch gun could not be sighted, due to the smoke box, so all aiming was done with the 11-inch gun since it did clear the gun port with sufficient clearance to sight it over the barrel.

Firing blind or not, there was nothing the Confederate States Navy could construct and float that could withstand the awesome, singular power of the 15-inch gun. While heavily engaged with C.S.S. *Tennessee* at Mobile Bay, the captain of the monitor U.S.S. *Manhattan* ordered the use of 55 pound charges to be used in the 15-inch gun. The ships were firing at one another within mere yards, spitting distance.

*The only shots which pierced the* Tennessee *were those fired from the* Manhattan, *Commander [James W.A.] Nicholson using a double charge of powder in a 15-inch gun. He ran the risk of exploding the gun, but proved that it could stand the double charge for a limited number of rounds.*[14]

By giving that order, Nichloson was directly disobeying naval regulations requiring the smaller 35 lb. charge. His decision to trust the gun, not regulations, in an immediate combat situation rapidly brought the Rebel ironclad's career to an end. The 15-inch shot cracked *Tennessee* open. Within an instant, the terrible effect of the 15-inch gun's solid shot crushed through six inches of iron plate and several feet of oak backing, showering the Rebel ironclad's interior with thousands of splinters of iron and wood. Inside *Tennessee* men were killed outright by showers of lethal splinters, wounded in horrible and tragic ways and knocked-out or rendered into semi-consciousness or shock.

In the early part of the Rebellion, an assessment of gun power versus armor resistance was offered in *Harper's Magazine*. The race between armor plate and the destructive power that could be directed to the penetration of that plate was questioned:

*Can a gun be constructed which will send a ball through any armor that can be made? and can any armor be constructed which will resist a ball from any possible gun? Theoretically, we must answer both of these questions in the affirmative, and so give the paradox: We can make armor which will resist any shot, and we can make guns that will penetrate any armor.*

*Practically,...we think the advantage lies on the side of the armor. We believe that our new Monitors will be, for all practical purposes, impregnable. We think the chances are a hundred to one that the turrets which we have described would not be injured by any gun yet constructed; and if additional strength should be required to repel the additional projectile force, that the thickness of armor can be increased more easily than the projectile force. Theoretically, there is no limit to either. Practically, there is a limit to both; and this, we think, will be reached in the case of the cannon sooner than in that of the armor."*[15]

In theory maybe, but in practice the 15-inch gun held the day. The gun was far from perfect. It required a crew of 14 to service, had a rate of fire of 1 shot every 5 to 7 minutes, and it was initially imperfect in its protective turret and great care was required to prevent a catastrophic bursting within the confinement of a gun turret. The navy, well aware of the dire consequences of a gun bursting in a turret, charged the gunners with keeping a keen eye on the huge guns. Among the several inspections needed to address regulations, a critical inspection required a wax impression to be taken internally, in the bore, to demonstrate any possible internal cracks or fractures in the iron:

*It was the custom in the Navy to take an impression of the vent of a gun after each day's engagement, for the purpose of ascertaining whether any cracks had been sustained by constant firing. This operation was usually performed by placing a piece of wax upon the end of a long rod and thrusting it into the bore of the gun, and carrying it against the inner opening of the vent. In the case of the 15-inch guns, however, this impression was taken by a messenger boy, who took the piece of wax in his hand and made his way into the gun, and thus brought away the desired impression. After a severe day's engagement upon a hot day in July, this boy nearly lost his life, through the carelessness of the gunner's mate, since he sent the boy into the gun before it had been sponged out, and the powder smoke from its last discharge had not been removed. The boy was consequently drawn out of the gun completely asphyxiated.*

*He was laid upon the deck in open air, and I spent an hour in resuscitating him. When he finally revived, he was so completely exhausted that it was necessary to send him away to hospital for a week or more.*[16]

There was no Confederate ship carrying a gun match for the pure fury and destructive power as the 15-inch smoothbore Dahlgren gun. That massive monster of naval gunfire reigned supreme in the Civil War and was, without a doubt, peerless.

*Gun crew drill.*
*Weighing in at only 760 pounds, the Dalghren boat howitzer was loaded with canister and kept at the ready. The little gun would provide a warm reception for anyone foolish enough to attempt boarding.*

# A FEW GOOD MEN

## John Worden

At the outbreak of secession, John L. Worden was a twenty-six year veteran of the navy, without a command, and sixteen years in grade as a lieutenant. It was a situation that was all too common in the prewar navy with its strict adherence to a seniority system of promotion. When the forty-three year old naval officer reported to Washington, D.C., in April 1861, he actively sought sea service, but took the first offer to come along. Gideon Wells, the new secretary of the navy under the equally new president, Abraham Lincoln, had a special assignment waiting for the right officer, and Lt. Worden was the one.

Secretary Wells entrusted Worden, an officer he considered "untainted by treason," to deliver direct orders to Captain Henry A. Adams in charge of the U.S. naval forces standing off Ft. Pickens, Pensacola, Florida. The captain was delaying landing troops to reinforce Ft. Pickens, and Gideon Wells wanted his order to land the troops and supplies delivered face to face to the vacillating Adams. Worden was given written orders for the captain and directed to read and memorize the text. He was further directed not to let the orders fall into the hands of the Rebels. Worden was to eat the message if he felt himself in the slightest danger, and to proceed to deliver the secret passages personally.

Lieutenant John Worden succeeded in delivering the message, personally; but not before having to obey his mandate fully by dining on the written communications. He was arrested by local Confederate authorities in the Pensacola area as he tried to secure passage out to the fleet. Upon his arrest, Worden was delivered to General Braxton Bragg, commanding the Confederate provisional forces in the area. There was no active, armed hostility within the country at the time. Fighting had not begun but conventions of secession were held in some states. Seven Southern states had declared their secession from the United States and began the formation of a loose Confederacy. Though his travel had been risky, and he had been stopped and detained, Worden realized that he could still successfully deliver the memorized communications from the Navy Department. Lieutenant Worden gave General Bragg assurances that his mission was peaceful, witness his mode of travel, and that he should be allowed to contact and communicate with Captain Adams out in the Bay. Not without doubt or suspicion, General Bragg relented, and under a flag of truce, Lt. Worden made his way out to the ships and delivered the direct orders to Captain Adams.

With his mission completed, John Worden made his way ashore and secured passage on the first train north. Adams, in compliance with the orders, started the reinforcement of Ft. Pickens and thereby alerted Bragg to the fact that he had been snookered. The general immediately ordered Lt. Worden to be found, arrested, and detained. It did not take long, for Worden was recognized and captured aboard a train in the Confederate capital of Montgomery,

Alabama, on April 13, 1861. John Worden was a prisoner of the Confederate States, and sequestered in the Montgomery city jail.

Although on a mission for his government under the direction of the Navy Department, Lt. Worden was allowed to remain in the city keep by the Navy Department without official moves to secure his release. President Lincoln's early policy of not doing anything that would by fact or appearances give recognition to the Confederate States government seemed to assure a long stay for Worden. The United States would not negotiate with a government that it did not recognize.

In the confines of the city jail, Worden's health began to fail as desperate efforts were made for his release through back door contacts. With his vitality nearly sapped, Lt. Worden was released through the concentrated efforts of his wife, fellow officers, and Flag Officer Lewis Goldsborough, commanding the North Atlantic Blockading Squadron. Goldsborough, having a few choice Rebel officers in his capture, arranged for a prisoner swap with the Confederate naval forces at Norfolk, Virginia. Worden was released from the city jail on November 13. He had properly endorsed the Agreement of Parole made out and signed by Major J. L. Calhoune, C.S.A., and immediately thereafter Worden was provided transportation by rail to Norfolk.[1] There, on the November 20, he was exchanged under a flag of truce for a Confederate naval officer captured at Cape Hatteras. The journey was over but his career was about to begin.

At the time of Worden's exchange, the Confederate naval forces were rapidly converting U.S.S. *Merrimac* into the Rebel ironclad C.S.S. *Virginia* in the captured Gosport Navy Yards. Worden did not know it, but in less than four short months, he would be back in the area, engaged in a fight to the death.

After release, Worden returned directly to Washington, D.C., seriously weakened by his ordeal of capture and imprisonment. However, he was determined to get command of a ship, any ship, and actively sought sea command. His lobbying efforts paid off as another offer was made that he knew was too good to refuse. Though still suffering the physical and mental effects of his mission South, he accepted the new command quickly. This was done even though

he was begged not to accept a new assignment so soon by, "...the protest of his physicians and the entreatment of his family."[2] The ship offered was U.S.S. *Monitor*. Worden had finally received a plum.

Commodore Joseph Smith, of the Ironclad Board, was in the unique position to offer command of *Monitor*. In light of Lt. Worden's recent service, and Commodore Smith being an old family friend, the commodore confided in the lieutenant: "This vessel is an experiment," he said, "I believe you are the right officer to put in command of her."[3] Worden, who pined to be a naval hero, now found himself to be exactly at the right place and the right time to receive command of what was soon to be a history making warship. His service, personal courage and his mental and physical fortitude afforded him a wartime jump ahead of other naval officers more experienced and his senior, who under the seniority system were rightfully in line for the command ahead of the pale and thin Worden. But fate, history and a family friend combined to pick this relatively obscure officer for the unknown task to come.

Lieutenant Worden reported to New York to take charge of his command which was being rushed to completion in wake of reports that C.S.S. *Virginia* was preparing to give battle to the U.S. ships in Hampton Roads. With the usual fits and starts accompanying any new ship, Lt. Worden oversaw the completion of the ship and started *Monitor* on her way to the mouth of the Chesapeake Bay. Worden, a gutsy man in command of a ship unlike any in the world, headed into the winds of history.

Disaster nearly befell *Monitor* on the way south. Pounded by a violent storm off the Jersey and Delaware coasts, she started to founder when her fires are all but extinguished by a monster wave that sent water crashing down the smoke stack and into the engineering spaces dousing the boilers and furnaces. Providence and Worden's quick thinking kept *Monitor* from going to the bottom on her maiden voyage. A crew member aboard on that trip remembered it this way:

*On their way down, probably on the night of March 4th, the* Monitor *telegraphed to the* Sachem *to come and take off the crew as the vessel was sinking. Just then the band which encircled the head of the* Sachem's *rudder slipped, and the vessel became unmanageable. It took perhaps an hour to secure it, and when the* Sachem *was laid along side the* Monitor, *it had appeared that the panic was past. A heavy sea had gone down the smokestack, the gas forced out from the furnace had overpowered the engineer and the assistant engineer, and left the engine in the hands of a young man just making his first voyage who became badly scared. By the time an hour had passed the fear had passed too, and they were willing to try their fate further, but the Captain told me that if the rudder band had held the* Monitor *would probably have been abandoned that night. On how small occurrences great events turn! In that case the* Merrimac *would have had no competent antagonist, and the Government might have lost control of Hampton Roads. The Captain, whose name I immediately forgot, seemed like a reliable person and I have no doubt he told me the truth.[4]*

The all volunteer crew, somewhat shaken by the experience of near disaster, brought the little ironclad into Hampton Roads in the early evening of March 8, 1862. C.S.S. *Virginia* had just retired upon completing her work of war for that day. The Rebel ironclad departed Hampton Roads with U.S.S. *Congress* and U.S.S. *Cumberland* destroyed and U.S.S. *Minnesota* hard aground. Admiral Franklin Buchanan, late of the United States Navy, in command of *Virginia* and her consorts, felt sure that the work of destroying more United States ships and assorted property could wait a continuance with the full light of the coming day. For now, Buchanan was wounded and needed attention ashore, and *Virginia* needed some quick and intensive attention to her wheezing machinery, leaking bow, where the ram was wrenched off, and a good resupply of shell to wreak havoc among the wooden fleet still in the Roads. No one looked back and saw the small Union ironclad arrive just as the action ceased.

Working throughout the night, Lt. John Worden had *Monitor* as ready for battle as she would ever be. With light of the next day and the approach of the Rebel ironclad, Worden steamed his first command out to face *Virginia*. The Rebel sailors were flushed by yesterday's victory and were spoiling for a continuation of their Yankee turkey-shoot. *Monitor* steamed into a battle which was now considered pivotal and marked the first fight between two armored ships of war.

In a fight that seemed endless, hours of battle came to an abrupt end in the sudden flash of a shell explosion right before Worden's eyes. He was temporarily blinded and his complexion peppered for life with black powder.

*Soon after noon a shell from the Merrimac's gun, the muzzle of which was not ten yards distant, struck the forward side of the pilot house (of the Monitor) directly in the sight hole and then exploded. Captain Worden was standing immediately behind the spot and received in his face the force of the blow, which partially stunned him, and filling his eyes with powder, utterly blinding him.[5]*

The shell had struck *Monitor* in her weakest spot. The resulting confusion in the pilot house caused the ship to be taken out of the continuing fight and into shallow waters. Attention was given to getting Lt. Worden into his quarters and under care while the executive officer, Samuel D. Green, prepared to reopen the contest. The lumbering *Virginia* withdrew in the direction of Craney Island and her support, satisfied that *Monitor* had withdrawn to the shallows seeking safety. But as *Virginia* retired she left behind, and untouched, the remaining ships

*Samuel D. Green, Executive Officer on* Monitor.

of the Union fleet and the Roads securely in Union control. The blockade of any Confederate waters would never come this close to being broken at any other time in the ensuing war years.

Lieutenant John L. Worden, suddenly a national hero, was showered with the thanks of a grateful nation. With accolades accorded and medical attention bestowed by the best there was, Worden recovered sufficiently enough from his blast wounds and exhaustion to receive command of yet another monitor, one of the new and improved Passaic class ships, U.S.S. *Montauk*. The sudden hero served well as the captain of his new ship, surviving point blank gun duels with Confederate fortifications, and a torpedo explosion that ripped the ironclad's hull and forced him to beach the monitor for emergency repairs. But before *Montauk* took a battering from Ft. Sumter and the other Charleston Harbor forts, Worden was relieved of command. He was too weak, his remaining strength seriously sapped by active duty. The worried Fleet Commander, Admiral DuPont, ordered John Worden to take leave from the fleet and to report home for a longer and more complete rest.

Although John L. Worden would never command another monitor after *Montauk*, he continued with a long and fruitful career in his beloved Navy. He was a veteran of just about anything that life could throw at him. But, regardless of his further successes and honors in life, all events subsequent to March 9, 1862, would in essence be anticlimactic. There would never again be anything to match that first command. To this day Lt. John L. Worden, U.S.N., is remembered for that one day of singular courage.

# Louis N. Stodder

Louis N. Stodder was one of the many volunteers to show up at the beginning of the war to serve his country in the capacity he thought best. He was appointed as an acting master from the state of Massachusetts the day after Christmas, 1861. Awaiting assignment, Stodder was assigned to U.S.S. *Ohio*, a harbor bound, 74-gun, ship-of-the-line, past her prime, but large enough to serve as a receiving ship.

Stodder without a doubt knew of the building of the Rebel ironclad and of the rush that was on by the United States to build ships to face the promised Rebel threat. The young master received orders to join the crew of the U.S.S. *Monitor*. There was little time for the men, or Stodder, to become accustomed to their ship and her workings, for she was sent south as soon as her early mechanical bugs were addressed and worked out. The weather was rough going south and at one time in the passage *Monitor* was prepared to be abandoned, but survived. Arriving on the late evening of March 8, *Monitor* prepared for the next day. Stodder was just as busy as anyone in the crew preparing for the unknown of the morrow.

The fight of the next day is world renowned. Stodder was in the thick of it in the turret. During the action, he made the mistake of leaning against the interior wall of the turret during a short lull in the firing. *Virginia* opened again on *Monitor* and a shell hit square on the turret, exploding and ringing the turret as a bell with concussion. Stodder "...was flung by the concussion clean over both guns to the floor of the turret."[6] The twenty foot flight knocked out the young officer and required that he be taken below where he remained unconscious for over an hour. His day was done.

*Admiral John L. Worden*

*Master Louis N. Stodder*

Stodder remained with the ship and the following actions to come. He finally returned, with *Monitor*, to the Washington Navy Yard for an overhaul in October 1862. While there, *Monitor* was a real celebrity, as this was her first, and only, public opening after the battle of Hampton Roads. *Monitor* was opened for public inspection for a day and the famous ironclad was assaulted by throngs of adoring and curious persons, all eager to walk her decks of glory. The people clamored up and down her ladders and through each and every passage way and open space available for inspection. Stodder recorded at the end of the day, "...there was not a key, doorknob, escutcheon—there wasn't a thing that hadn't been carried away."[7] The adoring public had done more damage to the ship than the Rebel shells.

Stodder shipped again with *Monitor* when she returned to Hampton Roads. *Monitor* was then ordered to Charleston, S.C., to prepare for an ironclad assault on the Rebel stronghold. However, the end of *Monitor's* fortune struck the ship in the form of a terrible storm off Cape Hatteras. As *Monitor* foundered from the beating waves, and the water in her engine room was over a foot deep and rising, Captain Bankhead ordered the large hawser holding *Monitor* to *Rhode Island* to be parted. In the howling storm the Captain raised his voice shouting, "...Who'll cut the hawser!" An imme-

diate answer came from the young acting master who seized a hatchet and climbed down the turret ladder onto the deck. He was followed by James Fenwick, quarter-gunner and boatswain's mate John Stocking. Clinging to the lifelines rigged around the deck, the men moved forward to sever the huge rope tying *Monitor* to her tow. Waves swept the flat deck with thunderous tons of cold salt water, slapping the men about. The sea was angry, and before the bow was reached, both Fenwick and Stocking were carried away into the boiling waters and into the darkness of a watery grave.[8]

Stodder, alone and fighting for his life in the dark and angry sea, reached the bow. Dropping firmly onto his knees he hatched the hawser and struggled for dear life as the towering waves rolled high above his head. Slashing through the last strand of hemp, Stodder flung aside the hatchet as the heavy rope parted. Exhausted, he fought his way back to the turret, and awaited the final order to abandon ship. It was a hero's job, done by a volunteer doing his duty.

The young volunteer survived the terrible night, and ten days later received promotion to acting volunteer lieutenant. He was awarded a command of his own, U.S.S. *Adela*, an iron hull, side wheel steamer whose most recent career was as a blockade runner. He remained in command of *Adela* for the rest of the war, serving his country well. When the end came, he walked away from the navy with an honorable discharge and the pride in having done his duty.

## John Payne Bankhead

John Payne Bankhead, last commander of U.S.S. *Monitor* was born in South Carolina. At the time *Monitor* floundered, on New Year's Eve, 1863, in heavy seas off Cape Hatteras N.C., John Bankhead was taking his ship to prepare for a naval assault on Charleston, the birthplace of secession, the land of his birth. However, the diminutive ironclad that changed naval warfare overnight was not designed for the open ocean. Even under tow of U.S.S. *Rhode Island*, Bankhead and his ship could not handle the brutal seas off Hatteras. Doing all he could, and nothing less, *Monitor's* commander ordered her

*John Bankhead, last captain of* Monitor.

abandoned. After hours of trying to save his ship, with the angry seas pouring in, her fires out, her pumps inoperable, the ship was rapidly settling in the pitching storm. John Bankhead was in the last boat to pull away from the doomed *Monitor*, unable to help or rescue the panic stricken clinging to the vessel as she slipped beneath the waves to her grave. John Bankhead suffered greatly from the battle to save his ship and his physical strength waned so much that he was ordered to New York to recuperate.

While in the city, Commander Bankhead was assigned to command of U.S.S. *Florida*, then being converted at the navy yard from a solidly built merchantman purchased by the Navy Department. Although his illness lingered and his strength was slow in returning, the progress on converting *Florida* was even slower. It was not until the second week in March that U.S.S. *Florida* got under way. When she weighed anchor, *Florida* had the new Passaic class ironclad monitor, U.S.S. *Nantucket*, under tow. It took a week of hard towing to reach Port Royal where *Nantucket* joined the South Atlan-

tic Squadron. It may have seemed odd to Bankhead to deliver this new monitor to the same safe harbor that was his original destination with U.S.S. *Monitor*, just a few months prior.

Bankhead's health never fully recovered, even though he continued in active service with *Florida*, U.S.S. *Otsego,* and his last command, U.S.S. *Wyoming*. That last command, *Wyoming*, Bankhead directed into the China seas looking for the Rebel raider C.S.S. *Shenandoah*. Although he sailed with the utmost dispatch, Bankhead failed to arrive in time to keep the Rebel raider from making her way safely back to England.

Bankhead's health continued to deteriorate; he was relieved of command and ordered back to the United States. While in passage, his conditioned failed, and he died on his way home aboard ship near Aden, Arabia.

John Payne Bankhead was but one of a special breed of men. These men were as solid in spirit and backbone as the iron warships they commanded, leaders and heros to generations now regrettably past.

Their lessons remain, however, to be learned by us all.

# A Messy Affair

At the age of twelve, young Samuel Francis DuPont received an appointment as a midshipman in the United States Navy, the start of a long and changeling career, full of promise. In the end, however, it left him old and bitter, estranged from his beloved Navy. Dupont was born near present day Bayonne, N.J. into a family rich with political influence, connections, and cousins enough for him to marry one, keeping the family close.

With the outbreak of the Civil War, DuPont served as head of the board whose mission was to conceive and set naval war strategy. In short order, he was offered command of the largest American fleet ever assembled, the South Atlantic Blockading Squadron (S.A.B.S.). Under his command the navy started the campaign to smite Charleston by first attacking and securing Port Royal, S.C. as a coaling and repair station. DuPont's actions gained him an admiral's promotion, public praise, and a vote of thanks from the U.S. Congress.

While in command of the S.A.B.S., the riff between Samuel DuPont and Secretary of the Navy Gideon Wells, was public. Wells had not made DuPont his first selection for command, but instead selected Andrew Foote, who had been making a name for himself on the Western waters. But Foote, who had been wounded in battle, repaired to New York City, and while preparing for the new command and resting his wound, died suddenly. With no commander, Secretary Wells was forced to appoint the very man he had tried desperately not to give the job to in the first place.

A large part of DuPont's mission and concentration as commander of the blockading force was not only to strengthen the blockade, but to force a passage into Charleston, birthplace of the hated Southern rebellion. To this end, he assembled an attacking force of seven Passaic class monitors and two other ironclads, the broadside gunned U.S.S. *New Ironsides* and the tower ironclad, U.S.S. *Keokuk*. Although Admiral DuPont was an officer of many years, his experience as a commander was limited.

As pressure from Washington built to attack, DuPont was hesitant, and suffered serious doubts about the power of ironclads to force their way into the Rebel harbor. His apprehension was freely communicated to whoever would listen. He complained almost endlessly about the numerous faults of the ironclads, including their serious want in construction. In a letter to Assistant Secretary of the Navy, G.V. Fox, DuPont penned:

> *I think these Monitors are wonderful conceptions-but oh! the errors of details, which would have been corrected if these men of genius could be induced to pay attention to the people who are to use their tests & inventions.*[9]

President Lincoln, well aware of the shortcomings of his commanders on land as well as the sea, gave his own personal opinion of DuPont to Secretary of the Navy Gideon Wells. In Well's office, Lincoln insightfully remarked to his secretary:

> *...[there is] but slight expectation that we shall have any great success from DuPont. He as well as McClellan hesitates—he has the slows....DuPont is everlasting asking for more...ironclads. He will do nothing with any. He has intelligence and system, and will maintain a good blockade. You did well in selecting him for that command, but he will never take Sumter or get to Charleston.*[10]

DuPont, prone to his own power cliques, was jealous of the inventor John Ericsson, his Navy Department cronies and their overall presidential favor, power and influence. DuPont had launched himself on the path of self destruction as his own thinly-veiled slaps at these powerful men curried him no favor and assured future problems. Assistant Secretary of the Navy, Gustavus Fox, far friendlier to DuPont than most in the department, and himself a proponent of the monitor myth, prodded the man of

*Samuel Francis DuPont*

the moment, DuPont, to make the attack. Fox pointed out that the attack was much more than a mere assault on the entrance to Charleston: "Finances, politics, foreign relations, all seem to ask for Charleston."[11]

The pressure was unbearable. Although uneasy with his task of breaking into Charleston with the ships he is assigned, DuPont sets the date of April 7, 1863, for the attack. Fox adds further to the urgency as he notes: "The people will have nothing but success and they are right."[12]

With the day of the iron assault at hand, the monitors, in line ahead, muddled their way into the outer reaches of the harbor to give battle to the defending Rebel forts. The flat bottomed monitors were very slow and extremely sluggish in answering the helm and, at times, almost unmanageable. To accommodate the firing of their guns with any chance of accuracy the monitors were anchored once in effective range to open fire. The Rebels, with foresight, had placed range buoys in the channels. Using their pre-sighted range markers the Rebel gunners rained down a hail of almost instantly accurate fire. The monitors were little more than targets allowing the effective Southern gun fire to exact a telling toll. With the exception of the broadside ironclad U.S.S. *New Ironsides*, the monitors and U.S.S. *Keokuk* were too slow in firing to effect any real damage or, most importantly, suppression of the Confederate cannon fire. The Passaic class monitors were each armed with a mixed battery: a monster 15-inch smoothbore and either an 11-inch smoothbore or 150-pdr. rifle.

The firing of the turret guns was only as rapid as the slowest, that being the 15-inch smoothbore, with a combat reload rate of up to 10 to 15 minutes. Anchored in place and firing slow, the monitors were unmercifully battered by the Rebel gunners, as though it was all a huge turkey shoot. By the time the signal was given to withdraw, the monitors were effectively unable to continue the engagement. The ironclad *Keokuk*, thinly armored, was so thoroughly riddled by cannon fire that it was hard to control the rush of chilled April seawater pouring in. The ship steamed slowly out of battle and anchored in shallow water, to continue efforts to keep her afloat. However, her damages were too extensive, and she sank the following day. The monitors were badly chewed up, but none were

in fear of being lost. The attack was a miserable failure, and Admiral Samuel Francis DuPont was in charge.

After the withdrawal before the Rebel forts was completed, Admiral DuPont ordered all the ironclad commanders to report to him aboard the flag ship. He wanted firsthand accounts of the operations, battle damage reports and opinions as to the possible renewal of the assault on the following day. By the end of the meeting, DuPont concluded he could not send the monitors back into the tempest of gunfire to try anew. It was a wise and correct decision, but his acrimonious relationship with Secretary of the Navy Wells and other "monitor men" did not allow acceptance of DuPont's logic and argument in defense of his decision not to continue the fight. As he had pointed out and the attack had proven,

> *...whatever degree of impenetrability they [monitors] might have, there was no corresponding quality of aggression or destructiveness as against forts, [due to] the slowness of firing...*[13]

There simply was not enough punch available in these ironclads to make the kill on a fort once the ship had moved in close to trade iron and black powder blows.

DuPont, by now, was convinced that his thoroughly critical opinion of the monitors was correct. Although right in his overall assessment, the admiral was hounded by louder than usual politicians, a misinformed public, and sensational newspaper accounts. As one New York paper put it:

> *One result of the Charleston fight will be to restore Beauregard to favor of the Southern people. Truly is he boastful, egotistical, untruthful, and wanting in tact, but he is currently the most marvelous engineer in modern times. By his genius and skill he erected batteries in Charleston harbor that would sink all the wooden fleets of the world did they come under fire, and he has succeeded, moreover, in driving back in disgrace the most impenetrable ironclad fleet afloat.*[14]

The paper's assessment of Confederate General Beauregard's skill in constructing the defenses supported the opinion that DuPont had formed earlier. For months prior to the attack, DuPont's staff had been working hard in making an assessment of the harbor defense. After countless observations and interviews with runaway slaves and deserters, Dupont's assessment of what lay before him was; "simply fabulous."

DuPont publicly criticized the folly of reliance on and faith in the monitors, but his presentation of the facts fell on the deaf ears of a wartime government, and people who had been singing the praises of the savior ship, ever since its David vs. Goliath fight with the ironclad C.S.S. *Virginia*. As for Secretary Wells, the culpability was clear:

*In Washington, the mechanism to achieve that victory appeared self evident—the new ironclads, whose capabilities after Hampton Roads seemed unlimited. To Wells and Fox the wish was the fact, but they failed to appreciate, as DuPont did, that a successful attack by a naval force alone was unlikely.[15]*

Admiral DuPont aggravated the open wound as he remained totally unapologetic, accusative, and critical of the monitors and all the men connected with the advancement of that ironclad class. Gideon Wells, acting on his own dislike of DuPont and using the groundswell of public and naval criticism for backing, lowered the boom on the admiral. Dupont had sought to defend his actions and failure based on a perceived weakness of the monitors, to which Gideon Wells commented in his diary:

*...he [DuPont]wants to lay his failure at Charleston on the ironclads, and with such a court as he would organize, and such witnesses as he has already trained, he would procure both Stimers and vessels to be condemned.[16]*

DuPont, relieved of command of the South Atlantic Blockading Squadron returned to his home in Wilmington, Delaware, to brood and fuss. His long service to his country continued slowly, as following assignments were to sit on committees and boards of no real significance. In Washington:

*...as far as the Navy Department [Gideon Wells] was concerned, his presumed animosity and subsequent involvement in Washing-*

*ton politics destroyed any possibility of further significant service.[17]*

Command of the South Atlantic Blockading Squadron was turned over to a junior-in-grade officer with very limited sea service, but with the right political connections, Commander John Dahlgren. Many other naval officers did not see Dahlgren as a good choice and expressed that they had little faith in the appointment. He had made his naval career based on his excellent, innovative work with naval ordnance, which in turn placed severe limits on his sea and command experience. In private correspondence, Commander John Rodgers noted:

*Dahlgren is coming out and I presume is now on his way—he has seen little sea service, and as far as I know he has never heard a shot fired in anger—He is promoted for his service on shore, and sent to command those who have had far more experience in the active duties of the profession—So goes the world.[18]*

*Commander John Dahlgren*

Overall, the new commander fared no better attacking Charleston with the monitors, but Dahlgren retained his command by remaining active, and not being overly critical, of the ironclad monitors and especially his superiors. Knowing when to speak and what line to walk made all the difference between DuPont and Dahlgren; they essentially did the same thing but met with vastly different approvals:

*...in May, 1864, the Admiral (Dahlgren) held a council of his nine ironclad captains touching on the feasibility of another naval attack on Charleston. All these officers expressed themselves ready and willing to engage in another attack with the greatest alacrity; but their judgement was against it. Only two voted in favor of the attack; and these were the youngest holding commands,—Lieutenant Commanders George E. Belknap and Joseph N. Miller; while seven voted in the negative, one of the seven being Commodore Rowan. If this prudence did not suit everybody, it was enough for the Admiral, that it was approved at the time by the Navy Department (Gideon Wells) and afterwards by Sherman.*[19]

When the monitors finally passed the batteries and steamed before Charleston, it was without battle. The advancing Union Army under General William T. Sherman approached the city from the south, but bypassed it, and caused the panicked evacuation of the city.

Samuel Francis DuPont, naval hero and pariah, in virtual retirement, bitter and broken, died on a June day in 1865 while on a trip with his wife to Philadelphia—not a monitor man.

# Commander George W. Rodgers

Anxious to get into the coming fight, Captain George W. Rodgers volunteered to rejoin his prior monitor command, U.S.S. *Catskill*, for the action. On August 13, with the early morning sun already bright and high in the sky, the ironclad steamer went into action against the Con-federate earthen and sand battery known as Fort Wagner. With the ship cleared for action and steaming slowly, *Catskill* came within 500 yards of the Rebel fortification and dropped anchor at 7:40. As the turret revolved slowly, the two huge naval guns were ready to deliver their fire into this den of rebellion. With several jerks and starts, the guns were lined up and the lanyards yanked clean and hard.

Captain George W. Rodgers was newly promoted to his current position of fleet captain, and served directly under his friend, Admiral John Dahlgren. Not wanting to miss out on the up close action, as his new station would normally demand, George Rodgers used his friendship with the admiral to gain his approval to return one last time to action. Rodgers was proud of his ironclad, the Passaic class monitor, U.S.S. *Catskill*, and he wanted to be there with his ship and crew in this upcoming engagement. Less than a month prior, a short note was received relieving Rodgers of his monitor command and assigning him to the position as chief of staff for Admiral Dahlgren. It was a plum assignment, no doubt, but one that would not be the position of action and individual command that Rodgers enjoyed with the ironclad. Friendships being what they are, Admiral Dahlgren consented to the request of his friend to fight *Catskill* again.

*Captain George W. Rodgers, killed-in-action.*

In the pilot house atop the turret, Commander Rodgers was squeezed into the cramped iron cylinder with three other men. With him were Acting Assistant Paymaster J.G. Woodbury, the pilot, Mr. Renton and at the helm, Acting Master's Mate Truscott. There was little feeling of apprehension as the fighting picked up and became thick and heavy. These men had been in action before and trusted the vessel in which they went into battle. Outside the eight inch thick pilot house the air was being churned by the flying lead and iron. Great fountains of seawater were splashing into the turret below from the water slapping, near-miss shots and the banging and rattling of shell fragments mixed with the thundering thunks of solid shots ringing the turret as a bell. The armored smokestack was pinging with regularity as the chips and slivers of iron and lead smacked the stack and skidded about the deck. Fort Wagner was "...firing very rapidly and using every conceivable form of projectile imaginable, from Minie ball to solid 10-inch shot."[20] Laying still in the water, the low profile of the ship offered but one real target, the turret:

*...it had been calculated that [the pilot house] were little likely to be struck fair by heavy shot. They were, however, just above the turret, and as the turrets were the only prominent targets at which to point guns, quite a good many shots struck the pilothouses, and they were severely handled.*[21]

It was not conceded in calculations that the ironclad monitors would be fought as stationary gun platforms. But for now, the men in the pilot house, though not at ease, nevertheless felt a degree of comfort within the massively built pilot house.

The anchored ironclad *Catskill* was almost too easy a mark for the 10-inch Columbiad under the command of Confederate Lt. J. Julius Alston. Within the sand and earthen fort, the Rebel gun crews were determined to score as many hits as possible, and to stop the attempt to silence their position. The Confederate gunners were well aware that the monitors had been defeated before and there was no reason to think otherwise at this time. Assigned as the gunner for the fort's powerful right side Columbiad, the young Southern lieutenant directed his full attention and duty to the monitor before his gun's muzzle, *Catskill*. All around Lt. Alston, shot after shot blasted from sea and land, bang and blasting, busting and killing. He noticed little of it as he concentrated on the monitor.

The pilot house, a cylindrical tower slightly over six feet in interior diameter, made very close quarters for the men directing the ironclad's shootout with the Rebel fort. Normally three men were the compliment required in the pilot house. Today, however, with Rodgers along, an extra pair of eyes peered from within the iron tower through the chiseled out and enlarged sight holes. *Catskill* was taking hits, but that was nothing new. Nothing was broken and the damage was not bad, yet. Beneath the pilot house in the turret, the 8-inch, 150-pdr Parrott rifle and the 15-inch Dahlgren smoothbore rattled the ship to its keel when they fired, adding bursting, rolling clouds of smoke and waves of deafening noise to the calamity of battle. Peering out at the enemy bastion, Captain Rodgers knew that each shot sent forward helped to blast another hole in the shaky Southern Confederacy.

In the open fort of earth and sand, Lt. Alson, determined in his right to freedom from Yankee oppression, sighted his huge gun carefully, oblivious to the hell bursting around him. With a deep breath, the lanyard is pulled taut, then firmly jerked, and the huge Columbiad jumped in recoil. At about mid-flight, Lt. Alston eyeballed the solid shot screwing its way through the air toward the ironclad. Its arch was perfect and the hit on the ironclad was solid and square, landing right on top of the pilot house. The Rebel gun crew rejoiced with battle cries wrenched from their parched throats. The unmistakable clang of the hit rang heavy in the air, sweet to the ears of the gun crew.

It was 8:20 when the pilot house took the fatal hit: "...a shot struck the top of the pilot house, shivering the inner plate and detaching three fragments of iron 3 by 5 inches in size."[22]

The devastation and carnage was instant. Inside the pilot house, Capt. George Rodgers and his friend, J.G. Woodbury, laid crumpled and ripped on the deck, both killed instantly by head wounds from the splintered chunks of iron. The pilot, dazed and wounded also in the head, stood in a stupor next to the dazed, slightly wounded helmsman. In the thick of blood, brains, confusion, and carnage, Lt. Commander Charles Carpenter took command. He ordered the dead and wounded removed, and charged to the care of the ship's doctor.

The pilot house was quickly inspected and flushed, re-crewed, and *Catskill* raised anchor and headed out of the fight. The ironclad, as rapidly as possible, came alongside the steam tug, *Dandelion,* out of range of the mocking enemy guns. Carpenter transferred the dead and wounded, and without further delay headed back into the melee; the dead would be hailed later, their honors accorded in due course.

The story of that day's action, and the death of George Rodgers, served as a further warning of a weakness of the Passaic class monitors; the pilot house. Bolted together from eight layers of overlapping one-inch plating, the seemingly protective and impenetrable tower was in reality a lethal post of duty:

*The plates of the turret and the pilot house were held together by numerous bolts, with the heads on the outside and a nut within. The blow of a very heavy projectile would make the nuts fly with great force within the turret, and the rebound of the plates would then at times withdraw the bolts entirely, but frequently they would stand out like the quills upon the fretful porcupine.*[23]

Fearful of this weakness being made public after the death of Rodgers, Admiral John Dahlgren sent a note ashore to the Union general commanding. The admiral was well aware that the Rebels read all the Northern papers, and that good intelligence was gained from the stories and reports. The weakness of the pilot house, made clearly known to the Rebels, would only invite further great gun marksmen to hammer away at the towers above the turret. His note reflected concern: "Will you request the correspondents of the press not to give the details of the death of Capt. Rodgers, as the information may be of assistance to the enemy."[24]

In earlier actions, aboard other ironclads of the class, other commanders and crew members had suffered wounds from the flying bolts and nuts within the pilot house. In the first action of the monitors against Ft. Sumter:

*...the Nahant took a frightful pounding. Shells hitting the pilot house caused the bolt heads to fly in all directions; the pilot was knocked senseless, the quartermaster was wounded, and only the commander was left in the pilothouse, with the steering gear disabled.*[25]

To save further injuries the navy retrofitted one inch iron sleeves into the pilot house on the Passaic class monitors, providing better protection from the flying nuts but not from a shot atop the structure. A Yankee style quick fix for the design flaw of the pilot house was implemented, "...by coiling heavy anchor-chain upon them in such a manner [so that] the effect of the shot would be chiefly expended upon the chain."[26] This action was much too late for Rodgers and Woodbury, but maybe it saved a life in later actions.

In this particular fight, the battle proved inconclusive, as did most of the fights in which the monitors faced Confederate forts up close. The monitors could take a pasting, but in return, the guns were just too slow to suppress the Rebel gunners' fire. Only the overwhelming broadside gunnery of the larger wooden vessels could suppress the Rebels with certainty. However, those same tender wooden walls kept the larger ships from closing with the Rebel fortifications enough to provide a knockout punch to the guns and crews. Clearly, the monitors could be stopped.

In his after action report to Secretary of the Navy Gideon Wells, Admiral John Dahlgren lamented the death of his friend George W. Rodgers and recounted the dead officers fine qualities. Although the admiral was not the only person to praise the fallen officer, Dahlgren perhaps said it best went he penned, "...the country can not afford to lose such men"[27]

# John Rodgers

*"...before breakfast we shall have in tow the Yankee Monitors"*

While attempting to destroy the abandoned naval base at Norfolk, Virginia, John Rodgers was captured and held prisoner by Virginia state forces entering the burning naval base to stake their claim to what had been an excellent Federal navy yard. The job of destroying the place was botched in a last minute rush, and Rodgers and several other officers and men did not try to effect their escape until it was too late. The prisoners were taken to Richmond as guests of the state of Virginia, but Rodgers was soon released. The governor of Virginia, with the concurrence of the legislature, decided it best to release the navy men since the state of Virginia was not at war with the Federal government. At this point in the war, a little thing like secession was not going to get in the way of gentlemen.

John Rodgers was born into a proud Maryland naval family on August 4, 1812. At the time of his birth in the family home at Havre de Grace on the Susquehanna River, his father was not at home. He was cruising against the British Navy during our second war of independence with the English crown.

At age 16, the young man began a distinguished career. Receiving an appointment as a midshipman, he followed his orders to join the Baltimore built U.S.F. *Constellation*, under the command of John's brother-in-law, Captain Alexander S. Wadsworth. For young John Rodgers, connections counted. His navy career was in its 33rd year when the Civil War broke out. Although a native of a border state, Maryland, there was never a moment of doubt as to his allegiance to the old flag. His friend and fellow Marylander, Franklin Buchanan, chose the new American flag.

After his release and return to Washington, Rodgers was directed to assist in creating the Mississippi River Squadron, which he did with zeal and vigor beyond his years. In succession, Rodgers was returned east to participate in the taking of the forts at Cape Hatteras, then ordered to take command of the ironclad, U.S.S. *Galena*. His new command was one of the three original ironclads authorized under the original Act of Congress to build iron warships for the navy. Of the three, *Galena* proved to be the worst in concept and execution as an ironclad, a role in which the ship totally failed.

The *Galena*, together with *Monitor*, attacked the Rebels' strong fortification perched atop Drewry's Bluff. Fort Darling was the only Confederate strong point between the Yankee ironclads and Richmond. The threat of C.S.S.

*Virginia* had been ended by the destruction of the Rebel ironclad by her own crew. After Confederates abandoned Norfolk to the Union forces retaking their navy yard, *Virginia* was left with no base of operations. As she was too deep in the water to be taken into the James River, she was fired and blown up to keep the Union forces from capturing her.

Just below the bluffs, the ship's channel had been completely obstructed by the Rebels. To remove the blockage would require the Union forces to engage and defeat the batteries atop the bluffs, which was an order not long in coming. The attack was a miserable failure, and *Galena* proved wholly inadequate as an ironclad. She was pierced with ease and with lethal regularity as Rodgers stood his ground, and tried to outgun the Rebels. By the end of the action, there were 33 dead sailors aboard *Galena*. The ineffective ironclad was soon stripped of her iron plating and completed the remainder of the war as the wooden hulled ship she truly was to begin with.

Because of his pluck and coolness under fire, John Rodgers received command of the Passaic class monitor U.S.S. *Weehawken* in January 1863. As her Captain he took her into the fight

*Captain John Rodgers, the ironclad killer.*

with Sumpter in April 1863, which again ended in the failure of the attacking ironclads. Though their stamina was second to none when it came to withstanding shots, their capability to take out a fortification was poor. This fight clearly demonstrated a weakness of the monitors, but the Navy Department refused to believe the truth.

In June, Rodgers was ordered to take his new command, *Weehawken,* in concert with U.S.S. *Nahant* to Wassaw Sound, to await the arrival of the Confederate ironclad, C.S.S. *Atlanta.* The Rebel ironclad had been converted at Savannah from an iron hull merchant ship, and by late May her immediate sortie was daily reported by a mixture of spies, deserters and runaway slaves. The powerful Rebel warship appeared in the early morning to give battle to the Union ironclad monitors awaiting her. The *Atlanta* was managed poorly in the first light and tricky river which put the ironclad hard aground on a sand and mud flat. Furious efforts were instituted to refloat the ironclad as Captain Rodgers directed his monitor to within 300 yards of the rebel ironclad taking his time and advantage of *Atlanta's* plight. Captain Webb of *Atlanta* watched the steady approach of the two monitors through the viewing slits in the ironclad's pilot house. In a vain attempt to halt the progress of the monitors, Captain Webb:

> ordered Lieutenant Barbot to open fire on her, thinking this would arrest her course and cause her to engage at the distance then between us; but on [Weehawken] came, unheeding my fire.[28]

Webb overestimated the power of his guns and underestimated the determination of Rodgers in his monitor to close and let force of arms settle the situation. At 300 yards, less than point blank range for the 15-inch gun in *Weehawken's* turret, the first shot was fired, "Using...thirty-five pounds of powder...and cored shot [of] four hundred and fifty pounds..."[29]

With telling effect, the *Atlanta* was ripped and splintered by the massive shot, and with four more shots following, the engagement was over before *Nahant* could bring a gun to bear. In his report of *Atlanta's* capture, Captain Webb's related the effect of one particular shot from *Weehawken*:

> ...the shot from the 15-inch gun [struck] our shield on a line above the port shutter, nearly abreast the pilot house, driving the armor through, tearing away the woodwork inside 3 feet wide by the entire length of the shield, causing the solid shot in the racks and everything movable in the vicinity to be hurled across the deck with such force as to knock down, wound and disable the entire gun's crew of the port broadside gun in charge of Lt. Thurston (Marine Corps) and also half of the crew of Lieutenant Barbot's bow gun, some thirty men being injured more or less.[30]

The casemate of *Atlanta* was one of the best the Confederates would build in the war, but it was not capable of neutralizing the terror of a monitor armed with 15-inch guns. The brief fight certainly made the Confederate Captain Webb appear somewhat of a fool and a braggart.

*The Rebel ironclad* Atlanta *at the Philadelphia Navy Yard after her capture by* Weehawken.

Not only had he mishandled the ironclad and run her aground before his enemies, but he had boasted to the crew just prior to going into action, that, "...before breakfast we shall have in tow the Yankee Monitors."[31] As it turned out, this was the only action of a monitor, one on one, with a Rebel ironclad, where the mortal contest was clearly decided by gunfire and the ability of the captains involved. Clearly, *Atlanta* was overmatched in both departments. Rodgers was even surprised by the briefness of the encounter and later stated:

*There had not been time to get up any blood or become in the least savage and when I saw the white flag so clearly as not to doubt, I only felt sorry for our prisoners.*[32]

The prisoners were later described by a Philadelphia newspaper reporter in very unflattering terms. It was a treatment that was not heaped upon the gentlemen officers of the ship. The reporter's description of the crew was as such:

*One cannot imagine a more villainous looking set of men than the same* Atlanta *crew. They are all Georgia "crackers," the poorest "white trash" of Georgia, with out education, or any thing in fact, which would entitle them to be called men, except that they have human form.*[33]

A somewhat larger, nonlethal struggle followed the capture of *Atlanta*. This time it was with the captain and crew of U.S.S. *Nahant*. They were insisting on a share of the prize money awarded, in the amount of $350,829.26, after *Atlanta* was adjudicated by a prize court. As with all captains of victorious warships, Rodgers got his sizeable portion of the prize money and was given an engraved silver service by the President of the United States for his stunning victory. Congress also provided him with a vote of thanks and the following words from the Secretary of the Navy:

*To your heroic daring and persistent moral courage, beyond that of any other individual, is the country indebted for the development, under trying and varied circumstances, on the ocean, under enormous batteries on land, and in the successful encounter with a formi-*

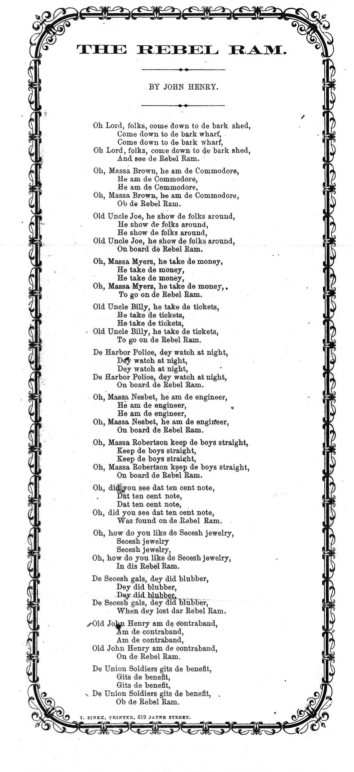

*While under repair in Philadelphia,* Atlanta *became a popular attraction. This poem was sold on board to the admiring tourist.*

*dable floating antagonist, of the capabilities and qualities of the attack and resistance of the monitor class of vessel and their heavy armament.*[34]

The capture of *Atlanta* was the end of John Rodgers' active Civil War involvement. He was promoted to commodore, and given command of U.S.S. *Dictator*, the uncompleted and much troubled pet project of John Ericsson, as she was nearing completion in New York. The *Dictator*, enormous by comparison to the original *Monitor*, was the passion of Ericsson who considered it to be the zenith of monitor design. The ship was a basic failure, having poorly designed and manufactured main bearings which were incapable of sustaining the ship's propeller shaft without failing.

At the end of the war, although overdue for shore duty, Rodgers accepted another monitor assignment. In command of a small flotilla, he was charged with bringing the large, double-turreted, U.S.S. *Monadnock* around the tip of South America and up to California. At the time of the voyage, Spain was at war with several of her colonies, and in particular, the new nation of Chili. George C. Remey, later a rear admiral in the U.S. Navy, remembered the arrival of Rodgers in the Chilean harbor of Valparaiso in the following words:

*About three or four months after our arrival, Commodore John Rodgers, with a squadron of vessels composed of the* Vandebilt, *Monitor,* Monadnock *(sic), the* Powhatten *and* Tuscarora, *came into port and remained... until the bombardment of certain portions of the city of Valparaiso by the Spanish fleet in April 1866.*

*About the same time the English Admiral, in command of the [English] Pacific fleet, arrived in Valparaiso with two British frigates. The sympathies of the British officials and sailors, as well as our own, were enlisted in behalf of the Chileans. It was well known that our commodore, John Rodgers, was much inclined to interfere with the bombardment by the Spanish fleet—by force if necessary. It was said, and believed, by the officers under him that he was very anxious to try the strength of the* Monadock *as against the Spanish broadside ironclad*

Numancia, *he having endeavored to enlist the British Admiral with joining him with his two frigates, but who, in my opinion fortunately, declined to entertain the proposition, on account, as he thought, of its being a matter between Spain and the other nations.*[35]

Rodgers had proven the monitors capable of delivering killing blows with 15-inch guns, and had proved that the larger monitors were capable of putting to sea, if constructed properly, and could, if required, steam from ocean to ocean and remain in position to offer battle to any ship foolish enough to test a monitor. Although Rodgers did not have the opportunity to have the monitor *Mondnack* batter the Spanish broadside ironclad, the threat was real. Also, it must be remembered that Britain had ironclads that were all broadside ships, and Rodgers knew full well that if the British admiral on station in the Pacific witnessed the destruction of a broadside ironclad by a monitor, the echoes of the battle would vibrate the walls of Parliament. The chance to demonstrate the power of a monitor to a world audience would not come true on this trip. Rodgers brought the small flotilla into San Francisco Bay and took pride in his association with the monitor class warships.

# Edward A. Decker

It was an assault as no other naval assault witnessed on this continent. Fort Fisher, North Carolina, was to be smashed by hundreds of tons of iron and assaulted by troops trying to end its protection of the Rebel port of Wilmington, the last anchorage and haven for blockade runners. It was the last doorway open to the outside world to bring supplies to the starving Rebel army entrenched at Petersburg, Virginia.

As part of the naval assault, Admiral David D. Porter ordered his ironclads to go in close and work over the Rebel guns, from a proximity that would be fatal to any of Porter's wooden ships in the massive fleet. For three days, the ironclads worked their way in close, and at 700 yards dropped anchor and attended to the day's business of shooting and being shot at in return.

Aboard U.S.S. *Canonicus*, acting master and pilot Edward A. Decker was attending to his duties in the cramped confines of the pilothouse. It was his job to bring the monitor and her two 15-inch guns to point blank range, and to do it in water that was at times less than a foot and a half under the keel. Within the massive iron pilothouse, Acting Master Decker knew full well that he was not safe from the Rebel cannon fire. Undoubtedly, that ten inches of iron was impossible to smash through with the weapons available, but nonetheless, several men had been killed in monitor pilothouses from a variety of freakish hits and faulty construction techniques. Also, if the monitor began to sink for any reason, escaping the pilothouse would be no easy task.

During this second assault on Fort Fisher, all four monitors stood their post at anchor and fired deliberately into the rebel fort. The monitors even tried reviving an ancient practice of bouncing the massive shots across the water:

> *Porter's monitors, closest to shore, tried with some success to "bowl" their 11-and 15-inch projectiles up the slope of the walls, figuring that a certain percentage would drop into Lamb's gun pits.*[36]

The massive balls were fired at such an angle as to skip them across the water then go rolling across the beach and up the sand walls of the fort. In return, the Rebel gunners took their shots at the ironclads and managed several times to hit the anchored *Canonicus* despite all the terrible iron and lead flying through the air. The turret took at least four hits by solid shots. Two men were stunned and knocked down by the impacts. One man in the turret was wounded by fragments passing through the sight hole in the iron wall and another by grape shot entering through the partially open gunport. Although well protected behind his wall of iron, Decker was not completely safe.

In firing, the Rebels demonstrated their knowledge of a weakness in the monitors—the turret top. Although the turrets "...required a building process involving the fashioning and assembly of 242 separate plates...nine feet long, three feet wide and an inch-thick...,"[37] the construction of the turret was weakest on

*Master Edward A. Decker*

the top. At sea, or in battle, the iron railing top of the gun turret was covered over with thin iron plates, leaving several hatches to gain access. Ventilation for the turret and the ship came through the turret top and any opening thereon and through the gun ports. Once the Confederate gunners had the range of the anchored monitors, they had no problem hitting the turret or exploding shells directly above. Any plunging fire, such as a large caliber mortar ball, could have smashed its way through the thin plates and played havoc with the crew and guns below.

Undoubtedly, the 10" thick pilothouse took its share of bursting shots and bullets from the fort. During the action, *Canonicus* fired 297 15-inch shells from her two guns in three days. And Decker, standing to his duty barely three feet above the two monstrous 42,000 pound guns, must have needed nerves of steel. In the official report of the action, the captain of U.S.S. *Canonicus*, George E. Belknap, gave direct, written recognition of his pilot for, "...performing his duties with his accustomed coolness and discretion...."[38]

The monitors were new and experimental. It required nerve just to look at these beasts. Edward Decker served in the most exposed position of the ship, in the pilothouse. It was well known that serving aboard a monitor was not an "ironclad" guarantee from harm, but Acting Master Edward A. Decker volunteered for duty, served well, and returned to his former life at the conclusion of the war. Honorably discharged on July 17, 1864, he faded back into the vastness of a nation preserved.

# Andrew P. Bashford

Our mundane lives are often touched, molded, and altered by small and large events, fate, which cannot be fathomed the moment they occur. It might be a predestiny affecting interconnected lives with the outcome for each individual as different from others as they are from one another. All things, great and small, contribute to this ever changing equation of our existence. Most events are ordinary, but some are pivotal; one such occurrence was the fate that struck the crew of U.S.S. *Patapsco* on the night of January 15, 1865. Scores died. Less than half the crew survived the catastrophic explosion that sunk the monitor in less than three minutes.

Among the ship's crew that evening in the waters of Charleston Harbor was a twenty-five-year old executive officer serving in his first real combat assignment. William T. Sampson was anxious for this duty, since the war had hastened his early graduation from the Naval Academy. After graduation, William had served aboard two sailing frigates in the coastal waters and rivers without facing the fury of any Confederate shot or shell. In July 1862 he was promoted to lieutenant, and had been returned to the Naval Academy as an instructor.

Now, the war was ending. It was but a matter of time, and William was anxious for the type of duty that his Scots-Irish blood and training had prepared him to perform. Maybe blockade duty was not necessarily exciting, but at least right here in Charleston Harbor he was firmly in the seat of the rebellion.

*Acting Master Andrew P. Bashford*

Also aboard that night was Acting Master Andrew P. Bashford. A native of Yonkers, New York, the twenty-six year old Bashford was married just three years earlier to Almira G. Waite of Newport, Rhode Island. Six weeks after their February 1862 wedding, Andrew reported to the Navy Yard in Boston, Mass., where he received a volunteer appointment as mate in the U.S. Navy. Also, shortly after the February nuptials naval history was forever altered by the fight between C.S.S. *Virginia* and U.S.S. *Monitor*. The battle and the subsequent intense news coverage of that naval spectacle were hot topics of conversation not only in the United States and the Southern Confederacy, but among the naval world powers who sharply recognized the portent of the two-day battle in Hampton Roads, Virginia. Andrew Bashford, described as "mariner" on his marriage certificate, would have been fully aware of the action and perhaps discussed the ramifications with his new wife. Andrew was initially assigned to the incomplete U.S.S. *Conemaugh*, a Sonoma class side wheel gunboat, as she was being constructed at Portsmouth. That was followed by his appointment as acting ensign on September 10, 1863, and assignment to U.S.S. *Oleander*, a small two gun side wheel steamer, and following, the Passaic class ironclad, U.S.S. *Patapsco*.

By January 1865, the war in Virginia had ground to a tactical halt and a mud covered, disease infested stalemate in the trenches before Petersburg. However, each day saw Union losses replenished with more men, while the Confederate troops suffered irreplaceable losses brought forth daily with static trench combat. Time was the Union ally, but the calendar of doom for their Southern enemies before them. To this end the Union navy had been instrumental, not so much by actual combat, but rather the endless hours upon days, heaped upon months and years, of blockade duty. Less and less with which to counter the industrial Northern giant reached the entrenched forces of secession. That giant ceaselessly pounded away, grinding down the war machine and fighting will of their brother foes.

Life aboard the blockaders was far removed from the glamour of the chase, and the sweet cash prize given for a captured blockade runner. For Lt. Sampson and the rest of the crew life could have been much better. Monitor duty was akin to penal punishment, doing time in an iron vault for the crime of joining the navy, a punishment of such a degree that today would surely and justly be considered cruel and inhumane. Aboard a monitor in the cool months,

> ...condensation ran in streams down the bulkheads, and it made everything from beds to shoes damp and mildewed. In summer, serving aboard a monitor was more like living inside a Dutch oven.[39]

Regardless, the responsibility was accepted by all on board as they attended their task on that ominous night. Twinkling in the distance were the dim lights of the Rebel city of Charleston. A mere 700 to 800 yards away stood the still lethal rubble of Ft. Sumter. Fate and duty came together for Lt. Sampson and Acting Master Andrew P. Bashford. It was a fate that selected a young lieutenant for a premiere life while assigning Andrew Bashford an important if not critical role in young Sampson's life. However, it was a role soon forgotten and ultimately passed over by history but for several lines in the official reports.

That night, U.S.S. *Patapsco* was attending to her dangerous bit of work, dragging for the fearsome torpedo, a crude contraption, primitive

*Ensign William Sampson*

in construction and execution, but nonetheless lethal. Just the previous August at Mobile Bay, Farragut's fleet witnessed a calamity visited upon U.S.S. *Tecumseh* by a similar weapon. That ironclad's destruction dispatched ninety-two men to their ultimate fate in a few horrible minutes. After passing Fort Morgan, the ironclad struck the underwater mine which opened a huge hole in her hull. Pushed by her huge propeller *Tecumseh* literally dived to her death. The torpedo similar to the ones *Patapsco* fished for in her early evening assignment. The cold, rusting ironclad slowly steamed and drifted to and fro in her deliberate and careful search.

Eyes scanned the horizon, darting in excitement to the fort and then back to a peering and straining search of the murky waters:

*The Patapsco had her torpedo fenders and netting stretched as usual around her. Three boats with drags...preceded her, searching to some depth the water they had passed over....[40]*

From his station on the turret top, the monitor captain, Lt. Commander S.P. Quackenbush directed the night's operations. With the captain stood Lt. Sampson, Acting Master Bashford and the quartermaster of the watch, no doubt they were all intense and focused upon the work at hand. Whispered words slid out of pursed lips and all conversation was short of expansive details. Time slowed and palms were wet, chilled with the night air. The air was fresh but provided little relief from the raw nerves knowing the water's hidden dangers. Eyes worked to identify anything in the water, breaking but for an instant here and there to glance heavenward in an appeal for salvation from this night's duty. In the ships directly ahead oars creaked and groaned, gently dipping in and out of the waters, slowly and carefully. The *Patapsco* moved forward. The duty was hell: "No one who has not witnessed it can appreciate the harassing nature of the never-ceasing vigilance with which monitor duty is sustained in this harbor...."[41]

Below the wardroom, the muffled rub of the torpedo was likely heard by the three officers passing the night in conversation. Then, "...there was a shock, a sound of explosion...A man in the windless room saw a flash and heard a sound like that of a shell near him."[42]

The officers froze, their eyes instantly flashed the truth of their last moments. There would never be a return home, because, "...the explosion occurred on the port side under the wardroom, blowing it up, so as to drive up the table and the three officers who were sitting at it."[43]

The explosion rattled the ironclad and the officers atop the turret. The *Patapsco* shuddered from stem to stern as the shock of the explosion rang the ship in metallic reverberations. A cloud of smoke rose and rolled over the port side, "...and in less than half a minute, the Patapsco's deck was under the surface."[44] Lt. Commander Quackenbush ordered the ironclads pumps started, but with reserve buoyancy allowing less than a foot of water to put her decks awash, the pumps proved useless against the flood of water erupting through the blasted-in underbelly of the ironclad. Rapidly realizing the blast was fatal, Quackenbush made his only possible decision.

*...the whole forward part of the vessel was submerged, and, there being no possible chance to save the vessel, I then gave the order to man the boats, but before even an effort could be made to do so the vessel sank to the top of the turret.[45]*

Men cursed and clawed their way through the dark inside the stricken ship. Panic pushed bodies from gun ports and up ladders through open hatches. Andrew Bashford and the quartermaster of the watch leaped from the turret top to the drowning ship's deck, half swimming, half churning their way to the boat rigged to the port side davit. Cries of death and the horrible sounds of the drowning ship filled the darkness. "It was only by great exertion that Mr. Bashford and the quartermaster succeeded clearing the boat from the head of the davits."[46]

*Lt. Commander S.P. Quackenbush*

With not a second to spare, the boat was freed of the sinking ironclad. Amid the clamor and loss of life, Lt. Sampson and Cmdr. Quackenbush struggled to reach the bobbing boat and the firm grip of Bashford and the quartermaster. Bashford's cool head and uncompromising hold saved the lieutenant and the commander from being sucked below by the doomed ironclad. With over sixty of her crew still aboard, U.S.S. *Patapsco* came to rest on the harbor bottom thirty-three feet below.

In that terrible night death did not visit Lt. Sampson. The aged and distinguished Admiral Sampson would die in his own bed in Washington D.C., on May 2, 1902 and be buried in Arlington Cemetery on the former property of the Rebel general, Robert E. Lee.

As for Andrew P. Bashford, his brush with fame passed. He continued on in the navy but was haunted by repeated physical maladies that kept him in and out of naval hospitals on a regular basis. At one point his health was so poor he was forced to leave the navy for seventeen months, from June 1868 until November 1869, when he was once again appointed mate, a rank he would retain until his death on June 30, 1889. His last active duty came aboard a rebuilt Civil War double ender, U.S.S. *Tallapoosa*. His health ended that service as he was granted sick leave April 12, 1883. The next three years was spent assigned to the receiving ships *Franklin* and *Wabash* at Boston. His death certificate is signed by Charles C. Carpenter, captain of *Wabash*. In part, the death certificate states the following:

*Patient had been repeatedly under treatment in the hospital for Rheumatism and Cardiac disease with albuminous urine. Was last admitted March 14th 1889 as with Rheumatism. On admission double pneumonia, albuminuria and mitral regurgitation were found. Condition of lungs improved after admission, but in other respects he lost ground. He died at midnight June 30th.* [47]

Andrew P. Bashford, Mate, United States Navy died in the U.S. Navy Hospital, Chelsea, Mass. He was fifty, five feet one inch high, grey eyes and grey hair and with a complexion described as "florid." His wife, Almira, moved from their house located at 18 Harvard Street,

Charlestown district, Boston, Mass., back to her childhood town of Newport, R.I. She applied for a widow's benefit and received a pension of $12 monthly until her death on September 4, 1904.

When Andrew P. Bashford died, William Sampson was the superintendent of the U.S. Naval Academy in Annapolis, Maryland. It is unknown if Sampson knew of the death of Bashford, the man who saved Sampson's life 24 years earlier.

# Barney Williams

Just north of Dallas, Texas, near the Red River in a small Texas town lie the mortal remains of a Yankee, Civil War naval veteran. It is not unusual to see graves of the fallen and of veterans, North and South, in this area, but this particular tombstone is slightly different. It tells us that this veteran, Barney Williams, was the last surviving member of U.S.S. *Monitor*.

Without a doubt, the American Civil War was vastly influenced by the huge numbers of immigrants who served in the armies and navies of the Union and Confederacy. Among the foreign born warriors, perhaps no group was better represented than the men of the Emerald Isle. No matter their reason for adopting America, these descendants of Celtic warriors provided the Civil War with men of honor, valor and a fighting spirit exceeded by no other ethnic group.

From Barney's obituary, he is related as being an immigrant from Ireland and a stonemason by trade. Apparently he was well thought of in his Texas and Oklahoma community and there was an expression of true sorrow on his passing in 1911. In trying to determine if he was, in fact, a monitor man, available references for crew members of the original *Monitor* were checked. Although there were plenty of foreign born men, from England, Austria, Sweden, Germany, Ireland, Wales, and other countries, there is no listing for a Barney Williams.

Plenty of sailors shipped under an assumed name, just in case the ship and its captain were not to his personal taste. The false name made it much easier to jump ship at the first opportunity, an ancient custom for ordinary seamen.

So it was thought that Mr. Barney Williams was one of the other Irish crewmen, but even that possibility was discounted. All the Irishmen were accounted for to their dying day, and not one was listed as in Texas or Oklahoma at the time of death. Of course, there remains the possibility that he was aboard another "monitor" and not the original one.

He has a government supplied tombstone, the paperwork for that stone was provided by Barney's son, but the application paperwork cannot be located currently in the government archives. Yet the person buried here could very well have done what is inscribed. Someone felt very proud of the fact that he did serve, if not on the original monitor, at least a monitor, and that made him special.

However, Barney Williams was not the last of the crew members to die. That honor belongs to another monitor man named Andrew Fenton of Vineland, New Jersey who died on April 18, 1945 at the age of 101 in the Old Soldiers' Home.[48]

*Headstone of Barney Williams.*

*Rare patriotic cover depicting the epic naval engagement between C.S.S.* Virginia *and Barney Williams' ship, U.S.S.* Monitor.

# WAR STORIES

## Repair Shops & A Hot Letter

As part of the Navy Department's push to punish and capture Charleston, South Carolina, plans were made for an ironclad assault on the harbor. Additionally, the blockade needed to be strengthened and sustained to keep the thousands of miles of coastline, rivers and inlets free of blockade running merchantmen. To succeed in this undertaking a staging area and supply and repair services were needed in the immediate vicinity, along the Rebel coast.

Several locations were considered, for without proper ship repair and refitting facilities the blockading fleet would have to reach north to Philadelphia or New York as the base for needed repairs, resupply and refitting. The distance to the Northern ports and the time involved in transit made that option unacceptable. After long reflection, Port Royal was targeted. Along with other strategies proposed by President Lincoln's "...was one to seize Port Royal Sound and its nearby island."[1]

Apparently Port Royal was perfect for the requirements of the fleet, only a few hours' sail from either Charleston to the north and even closer to Savannah, to the south. Plans for the assault and capture of the anchorage and its surroundings were made secretly. In a combined operation with the army, the Rebel forts guarding the harbor were overwhelmed by force of arms. Precious little time was wasted as Port Royal soon became the lifeline of the South Atlantic Blockading Squadron:

> With Port Royal under Union control, blockading vessels could be supplied, repaired, and fueled there. Its capture gave the Union naval forces control of the coast from above Georgetown, South Caroline, to New Smyrna, Florida, with the exception of Charleston, and also provided control of most adjacent inland waterways.[2]

By July 1863, when Pierre Giraud wrote the following letter to his brother, the Federal navy was still outside Charleston, unable to enter and capture the birthplace of secession. Giraud was serving aboard one of the Passaic class monitors, U.S.S. *Montauk*, having entered the sea service as a volunteer from his native state of New Jersey. Acting Master Giraud joined early in the war and had worked his way aboard the ironclad monitor commanded by John Worden. While aboard *Montauk*, Pierre's gallantry in action won him a promotion to acting volunteer lieutenant and the personal accolades of the ship's captain, John Worden and John Fairfax, a later captain of the same ship.

Giraud later transferred into the Gulf Squadron and joined Admiral Farragut's fleet in the fight at Mobile Bay in August 1864. In that action, the Confederate ironclad ram, C.S.S. *Tennessee* was battered into submission by the Union fleet. After the firing ceased the defeated Rebel ship lay still in the water, surrounded by her masters. The Union boys boarded their prize to claim her for Lincoln and the Union. They tended the wounded and made haste to transfer the Rebel crew off the ship. The wounded Rebel fleet admiral, Franklin Buchanan, was resting, as best he could in his quarters aboard the ironclad. Lieutenant Giraud was assigned by Farragut to receive Buchanan's sword. Buchanan later recalled the encounter:

*Captain Jones [of the C.S.S. Tennessee] did not deliver my sword on board the [U.S.S.] Hartford. After the surrender of the Tennessee, Captain Giraud [sic], the officer who was sent on board to take charge of her, said to me that he was directed by Adm. Farragut to ask for the sword, which was brought from the cabin and delivered to him by one of my aids.[3]*

After accepting the sword on behalf of Admiral Farragut, Lt. Giraud was given the honor of temporary command of the captured Rebel warship.

However, what stands out today about Lt. Giraud's letter of July 1863, is the fact that it survived at all. What makes this letter unique is this distinctive paragraph:

*By the way, I went up to Beaufort on Sunday with a few friends. Had a big time. Went to Church in the afternoon. Made love to a pretty yellow girl and got in a row with a Lieut of a Black Reg. Revolved my turret & let him have a 15 inch Shot. Accepted his apology and left, to take a horse back ride with a Friend, got caught in the rain, wet through, & in that condition returned to our steamer, arrived on board the "Montauk" in due time, satisfied in our minds that Beaufort is a gay place.[4]*

Although an interesting passage for the casual reader as well as the historian, the letter clearly establishes that the small village of Beaufort, S.C., was a place of "rest and relaxation" for the men of the fleet and provided services beyond those needed to sustain the ships alone. The needs of monitor men—drinking, fighting, horseback riding, prostitution, church, and other activities were readily available to comfort, console, and relax the ironclad warriors of the fleet.

It is easy to talk about the heroes and the average men who serve their country in its armed struggles. We know the stories well—their deeds of glory and sacrifice. But it is rare that we have an uninterrupted, unedited

*The U.S. Navy turned old warships into repair shops. These were needed to maintain the many ships and monitors of the blockading fleet. This repair shop was near Port Royal, S.C.*

glimpse into what made the heroes and the average men tick, to see something of their lives beyond the deeds of glory. The letter of this lieutenant, a hero in his own right, opens a small door for us to peek into the unseemly side of military life that provides relief from the pain of campaign and the gut wrenching loneliness that it brings, day in and day out.

> *U.S.S. Montauk*
> *Port Royal S.C.*
> *July 3/63*
>
> *Dear Brother*
>
> *As the Argo sails tomorrow I take the opportunity to drop you a few lines. I should have written you before, But it has been so remarkably dull with me. I had nothing to write about. We are now anchored about five miles from Hilton Head under repairs. The rebel ram Atlanta is at anchor near us. I was on board of her a few days ago. She is a very formidable craft and I think her Captain made a very poor fight of it. I wish it had been our good luck to have captured her. If you recollect we watched her for some six weeks when on the Ogeechee. Her captors will make a very handsome thing out of her in the shape of Prize money. We are making great preparation for another attack on Charleston, which event I think will come off in September. In the mean time I expect to pay you a short visit. That is if Captain Fairfax is successful in his application to the Admiral in my behalf. Captain F. thinks a great deal of me. I like him much better than I did Worden, Captain W. did not treat his officers right he should have had us all promoted. We helped to build his reputation, and he has neglected us, All on board feel very much hurt at this shameful treatment. I have a very good letter from him Which I will send to the Hon. Sec. of the Navy, on my return to NJ and with one from Captain F. I think I will be able to obtain my promotion, which I think I am Justly entitled to.*
>
> *The weather here is very warm, we are almost smothered on board the "Montauk". We cant get a thermometer long enough to measure the heat. Hard Story but never less true. By the way I went up to Beaufort on Sunday with a few friends. Had a big time. Went to Church in the afternoon. Made love to a pretty yellow girl and got into a row with A Lieut of A Black Reg. Revolved my turret & let him have a 15 inch Shot. Accepted his apology and left, to take horse back ride with a Friend, got caught in the rain, wet through, & in that condition returned to our steamer, arrived on board the "Montauk" in due time, satisfied in our minds that Beaufort is a gay place.*
>
> *Am going up again in the morning to spend the 4th their is to be a review of all troops in the department, amounting to about 10,000 men. We expect to have a very nice time. I wish you were to do with us. I went to Hilton Head yesterday, I spent the day there.*
>
> *We expect Admiral Dalghren here in a few days to relieve that old Humbug DuPont. I wish Foot had not been taken sick. He knows how to fight & would lead us right into Charleston. I have a great deal to tell you about our attack on Sumter but must defer it until we meet.*
>
> *I have received papers from you by nearly every Steamer for which you have my sincere thanks.*
>
> *Hoping Soon to Shake you by the hand*
> *I remain your Affectionate Brother*
> *P Giraud*
>
> *PS Remember me to all the Family and inquiring Friends*

# Inside A Monitor

If the monitors were anything, they were machines of war perfectly built to one purpose, and as such they did not pretend to address, to any real extent, the comfort and safety of the crew. There were few, if any, amenities, and shipboard life for an enlisted man was nowhere near bare minimum standards today. There was always a manpower shortage aboard these machines and the service was so vexing and dangerous, Gideon Wells authorized an increase in pay for the monitor men participating in the early attacks on Charleston. In part, the Secretary of the Navy wrote:

> *...in consequence to the nature of the vessels in which they are employed, their wages will be considered as increased by one-fourth... This increase will continue so long as the peculiar service last, and is to be confined to the enlisted men serving in the monitors engaged in the attack [of Charleston].[5]*

Although authorized bonus bucks for their service, the duty exacted a return rate higher than the invested pay could compensate.

The Passaic class monitor, U.S.S. *Nahant*, was not unusual in her experience with crew sickness, exhaustion and the disabilities of combat fatigue. In her first eight months of commissioned service, with only four officers remaining from the original crew,

> Nahant *had received forty-one replacements in one draft to fill to strength a crew of only seventy-five. All four of the engineer slots and the coal heaving ratings had turned over an average of three or four times.*[6]

Sickness abounded in the crews as the men suffered through seasonal changes in Southern waters where, "...life below the water line of an artificially ventilated vessel in a season and in latitudes where outer temperatures could fluctuate between forty and eighty degrees gave [the doctors] more sick traffic than usual."[7]

Crew berthing was located near the center of the ship where the men slung their hammocks from the overhead just as they would on a larger, wooden, man-of-war. However, berthing below the water line in an iron ship had its own unique qualities:

> ...in cold weather, serving in a monitor was like living inside a well—condensation ran down the bulkheads and it made everything from bed to shoes damp and mildewed. In summer,...a monitor was more like living inside a dutch oven. Morale was... bad aboard ironclads.[8]

In addition to the malaise brought on by the ship's condition, the fact that these men were fighting on an ironclad did not assure them freedom from death during combat. There was apparent safety behind the thick iron walls of the turret and the pilothouse, but death and wounding were not rare. The mere fact that these ships were "ironclads" tended to draw a heavy and concentrated fire from the Confederate batteries. The monitors would move in to almost point blank range to engage the Rebels, a place where no wooded ship of the fleet had a prayer of survival. The pounding received from large Confederate rifles and smoothbores of up to 10-inch caliber, gave the monitors much more of a beating than they could return. But their closeness allowed them a chance for that one well-placed shot necessary to take a Rebel gun out of action.

The U.S.S. *Catskill*, in one single engagement with batteries on Morris Island, withdrew from the inconclusive firefight with two men wounded in the turret, a brain concussion and a shrapnel wound from fragments entering the gun port, five officers and men unfit for duty from heat exhaustion, and another unfit due to a fall through an open hatch. This details a 15% casualty in one action alone. Such a rate could not be sustained for any length of time before the ship would be unfit for duty.

When going into action, the monitors were closed-up tight, all hatches battened down, stanchions cleared, ship's boats released and awnings struck below. Ventilation for the interior of the ship came through the turret. The top of the turret consisted of gratings through which the air was sucked below by the blowers in the engineering spaces. This arrangement worked most of the time but caused problems when the ship went into battle. The discharge of the turret guns created huge billows of acrid gunpowder smoke, which in part was drawn back into the turret by the ventilation.

> *Everything be made ready above and fastened down, it is dark as the blackest night, candles put out and lantern lit, every man at his station.... The men and officers below...strip off everything except pants and shoes. The thermometer ranges up to 95. The smoke comes...at every fire [of the guns] and is so thick in a few hours you can cut it....*[9]

No doubt the interior of the ship, below decks, was a place and time where good men soon learned their limits. Dark, extremely hot, stripped of clothing and fighting for breath in an atmosphere thick with choking smoke and, "...when shot and shell passed over...we can hear them scream like demons...."[10] Truly, a small touch of hell.

Discipline aboard ship was necessarily strict, but for the most part, the men were treated in a fair and consistent manner, with punishment meted out befitting the offense or the misdeed. Again, there were times when treatment and justice took a roundabout path.

An ordinary seaman, Thomas Thompson, filed a complaint with the Navy Department alleging abuse and maltreatment while serving aboard U.S.S. *Montauk* on March 9, 1863. The abuse was ascribed to Acting Master Edward Jones. When the squadron commander queried the shipboard surgeon, the doctor's statement, in part, read:

> *Thomas Thompson, ordinary seaman, contracted orchitis on the 10th of March, and is still suffering from the effects of the above disease. Having been exposed to cold and wet on the previous day, I am of opinion the disease originated from the above exciting causes.*[11]

Apparently, the seaman was dissatisfied with the surgeon's opinion and appealed. Orchitis is an inflammation of the testes and is described in a modern medical dictionary with, "The disease is marked by pain, swelling, and a feeling of weight. It may occur idiopathically, but is usually due to gonorrhea, syphilis, fiberial disease or tuberculosis."[12] The doctor was questioned by a board of inquiry and admitted that he had never treated or even read of a case of orchitis caused by exposure to cold or wet. With this revelation, the value of the seaman's contention that he was "kicked and abused" greatly increased. The investigation concluded, "...the statement of the medical officer was given for the purpose of screening an offender...."[13] Based on the conclusion, both Acting Master Edward Jones and Acting Assistant Surgeon W. H. Harlin were dismissed from the Navy. The dismissal order concludes with a very forthright paragraph:

> *Persons enlisted in the naval service may be assured that their complaints of maltreatment, properly made and forwarded, will receive due attention from the Department; and that the laws enacted for their protection will be strictly, and, in such cases as this, summarily enforced.*[14]

Seaman Thompson, despite his bout with orchitis, remained in the navy and even joined the crew of another monitor, U.S.S. *Canonicus*.

*Inside of the turret on the monitor* Montauk. *This drawing gives a false impression of space within the turret that was not the case.*

While there, he visited another surgeon after his ship participated in the bombardment of Rebel batteries at New Inlet, near Wilmington, N.C. On this visit, his disability was reported as: "Thomas Thompson, seaman, contusion left foot, caused by recoil of a gun."[15] Seaman Thompson was again too slow. But this time he stood in the way of a recoiling 20 ton gun and not a size eight boot.

A good illustration of accommodations made for officers was written by an acting assistant paymaster, a junior grade, volunteer officer aboard U.S.S. *Weehawken*. In a letter to his sister, he relates:

*My room is 8 feet by 6 feet 4 inches. I have in it a large mirror, black walnut frame a black walnut desk reaching up to the deck, 7 feet high, my berth is made of black walnut and drops down or fastens up like a child's crib on the side. Under my berth I have six fine large drawers in which I keep my clothes, my wash stand is of black walnut, I have two large pitchers, one small pitcher, one large mug, a soap dish tooth brush dish and one large slop jar all made of stone china and on each piece in large gilt letters is "Weehawken". I have splendid rich curtains to draw around my berth and in front of my door, each suspended by large brass rods, my floor is covered by a nice oil cloth bound around the edges by thin strips of brass and add a nice little camp stool to the list and you have all the furniture in my room.*[16]

The letter gives the impression of a small room, packed with built-in creature comforts, and a large slop jar, that any officer would be proud of calling home. The young officer from New York state also speaks of his hired help late in the letter:

*I neglected to say I have a fine black fellow by the name of Bailey about 20 years to take care of my room, bring me fresh water of which we have plenty, call me in the morning and black my boots & wait upon me at the [dinner] table, for all of which I give him 50 cents occasionally or a plug of tobacco.*[17]

The black man, most likely a runaway slave who found employment aboard the monitor, probably served several officers at one time. The pay, even for those days, could be considered cheap. At least he was free to enjoy the plug of tobacco as he deemed fit.

Without a doubt, the monitors were a breed apart, an experiment in naval architecture that essentially rewrote the book on naval warfare. Life aboard these experiments was as new and unique as the ships themselves.

# Puritan Parson Foote

Andrew H. Foote, a Connecticut Yankee, spent his spiritual and professional life in duty to God and the country. By age 56, Foote had earned the rank of admiral, and had done his holy best to drive the evils of alcohol from the daily sustenance of sailors in his beloved navy. Foote worked tirelessly in his assignments, but his zeal and passion were reserved for two items: combating the slave trade on the West African coast, and temperance. As executive officer aboard U.S.S. *Cumberland*, Foote worked for over a year building a temperance movement aboard ship. His efforts paid off and the *Cumberland*, under Commodore Joseph Smith, became a temperance ship, the first in the U.S. Navy. This was exceptional in a time when opening the spirits locker was normal, and a welcomed event in the daily routine of a man-of-war. It was custom.

With ceaseless effort, the fruition of Foote's work toward naval temperance came to bear with an Act of Congress on July 14, 1862. Except for medical purposes, alcohol consumption aboard U.S. Navy vessels was banned effective September 1, 1863. As due compensation for this loss of a sailor's daily ration, Congress authorized payment of an additional five cents a day. For those who looked forward to the afternoon snoot, the five cents was probably a poor recompense.

On Sunday, March 9, 1862, during the point blank pounding between U.S.S. *Monitor* and C.S.S. *Virginia*, a break in the action was precipitated by *Monitor* shearing off into shallow waters. She needed to resupply the turret with shot and shell, and the safest place to do so was in the shallows where *Virginia* could not follow with her 23 foot draft. As the work was going

*Commodore Andrew H. Foote*

on, the ship's captain, Lt. John Worden, authorized a fortification of the men by awarding a spirit ration during the lull. The order was passed to Acting Assistant Paymaster William F. Keeler to break out the whiskey. Keeler, a temperance man himself, found the instructions not to his personal liking, but carried them out as ordered:

> *Once during the fight I opened the spirit room by order of Capt. Worden & dealt out to each man half a gill of whiskey, & if liquor ever does good to any one & is ever useful it must be on some such occasion.*[18]

With turret replenished and the liquor locked up, *Monitor* returned to pounding *Virginia* with underpowered shots from her guns. This action, the battle, and the booze break, made U.S.S. *Monitor* the first modern warship, and perhaps the only ironclad, in the American Navy to take such a break. Although the law did not stop the drinking of spirits aboard ship, especially among officers, it ended a naval tradition rooted in ancient times.

As for Andrew H. Foote, his boyhood friendship with Secretary of the Navy Gideon Wells afforded Foote an early opportunity to make his war reputation, which he did in fine but almost reckless style. Captain Andrew Foote, commanding the Mississippi River Squadron, blasted out his Civil War reputation with fierce fights on the Western waters, using the early river ironclads to successfully attack and defeat Confederate forts in combined operations with the Army. While engaged in the attack on Fort Donalson on the Cumberland River, Captain Foote was wounded in the arm and left foot. A Confederate shot, plunging down from the fort forty feet above the river, pierced the pilothouse, killed the pilot, and wounded Foote.

His wounded foot did not heal, and Captain Foote left his command on May 9, 1862, to convalesce. The squadron command evolved to Captain Charles Davis, while Foote nursed the open wound. As a reward, Gideon Wells saw to Andrew Foote's promotion to admiral, effective July 16, 1862.

Following the bitter defeat of the ironclad fleet before Charleston, S.C., in April 1863, Admiral Samuel Francis DuPont was relieved of command of the South Atlantic Blockading Squadron. Again, Gideon Wells selected his old friend for the duty of replacing DuPont, and to effect the fall of Charleston. The temperance minded man of God, Admiral Andrew H. Foote, never reached his new command and his chance to effectively employ the monitors, for he died suddenly of complications while in New York City.

# An Enemy's View

For several years, Francis M. Hall, a young Confederate assistant engineer, spent untold hours attending to the mounting damage visited upon Fort Sumter and Morris Island. Constant attention to their combined destruction was the sole purpose of the Union ironclad fleet that spent much of its operational career before the harbor entrance to Charleston, South Carolina. Huge solid shots of 15-inch caliber lofted through the air slow enough to watch, and duck. Smaller 11-inch and 9-inch shot rifled through the humid air in flatter trajectories, smashing brick and mortar, redistributing rubble from previous blastings, and killing the occasional unlucky defender. In this stir of war, it was the

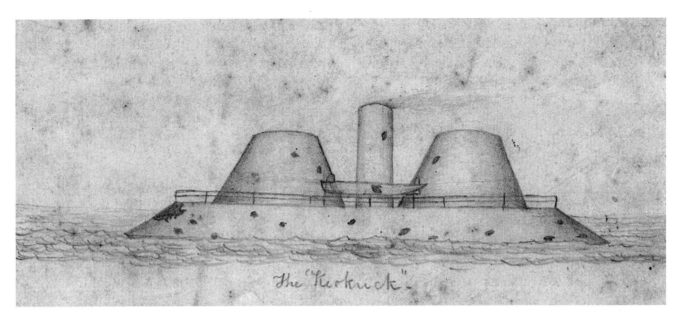

The "Keokuck".

*A Passaic class monitor (below) and the U.S.S. Keokuk (above) as drawn by a Confederate Army Officer.*

One of the Monitors which participated in the attack on Charleston, March 7th 1863.

engineer's job to maintain the Confederate positions as viable points of resistance that could stop the ironclads from forcing an entrance to the Rebel seaport. Lieutenant Hall and his contemporaries did a credible job.

When several openings became available for engineers in the Provisional Army of the Confederate States (PACS), the war-wise Lt. Hall collected numerous letters of recommendation attesting to his ability and honorable service. After posting his recommendations and letters of availability to the chief of engineers, the young lieutenant also wrote directly to Rich-mond, Virginia, seeking the position. In his letter dated February 11, 1864, from Fort Sumter to William P. Miles, a member of the Confederate Congress, Hall described his duty, in part:

*...I have already two years experience in the field, and have borne my full share of the toils and dangers of the siege of Charleston both at this post and on Morris Island. I was ordered to Fort Sumter on August the 29th and volunteered to remain at there (sic) during the siege and in accordance with the act have been stationed here ever since.*[19]

During this duty, Lt. Hall took an interest in the iron ships in the harbor and stole enough time to produce pencil drawings of the vessels. Two exist today, and they provide a view of the ironclads as seen by the enemy, by the people on the receiving end of the huge cannons carried by these iron monsters of the sea.

The first drawing is of a twin-towered vessel, U.S.S. *Keokuk*. This vessel was one of a kind, not a monitor, for the somewhat igloo shaped towers did not rotate, as would a turret, and the ship's armor was decidedly thinner than a monitor. Woefully armored, almost every heavy Confederate shot that hit her punched a hole in *Keokuk's* hull.

> *Kekouk was struck ninety times, nineteen shots pierced her armor at or below the water-line;...and the vessel was with great difficulty kept afloat until the next morning, when she fell over on her side and sank at the lower anchorage.*[20]

The drawing clearly shows the beating *Keokuk* sustained during the Federal assault upon the outer defenses of Charleston on April 7, 1863. It must have been made shortly after the assault, as the wounded ship sank within hours of withdrawing before the forts. The shot hole representations in the drawings graphically depict the beating that caused the mortally wounded ship to sink.

The second drawing, done on the front of an envelope, shows no such damage as visited upon *Keokuk*. This vessel is decidedly a Passaic class monitor, one of seven that took part in the same attack with the stricken *Keokuk* and the broadside ironclad, U.S.S. *New Ironsides*. It depicts a proportionally exaggerated turret and smokestack. Since the turret and smokestack were the only true aiming points for a gunner from hundreds of yards away, it makes sense that the drawing represents what the defenders faced. Possibly, it also represents admiration for the pounding they withstood, receiving close to 600 total hits on all the ships, and thus viewed as "larger than life." Of course, the singular gun port is incorrect, but that probably mattered little to a young officer of engineers.

Assistant Engineer Hall received his promotion, but more important, he left a legacy with his drawings. His unique sketches are witnesses to a time and place long removed, to people torn asunder by the lack of compromise, and to the inventions of persuasion and destruction they visited upon one another. Truly, the past is prologue.

## Threat From Below

The monitors in Charleston Harbor were kept busy by an unnerving vigil as the Confederates introduced several frightening new weapons of war. The semi-submersible "Davids," and a new, fully submersible submarine, caused severe consternation in the Union blockading fleet. Particularly concerned were the monitors, for their station was at the inner ring of that blockading fleet. Under Rear Admiral John Dahlgren, the South Atlantic Blockading Squadron conducted its dangerous work with a bevy of wooden warships, several monitors, and the broadside ironclad, U.S.S. *New Ironsides*. The ironclads, powerful world class marvels of American naval architecture, suddenly discovered that they were more vulnerable to the new Rebel vessels, armed with "torpedoes," than anything the Confederate surface fleet could fire in broadside.

Commander Daniel Ammen of the monitor U.S.S. *Patapsco*, wrote to his friend, Commander C.R.P. Rodgers, that the new Rebel vessels were designed "...for the purpose of blowing us all up by means of a newly invented detonating torpedo."[21] Charleston Harbor was now made more perilous by these answers to the mighty ironclads.

Admiral Dahlgren, commanding the South Atlantic Blockading Squadron, in a letter to Gideon Wells, Secretary of the Navy, dated January 13, 1864, expressed his concerns and precautions based on intelligence he had received on the Rebel boats. The letter was written after the October 1863 attack on the U.S.S. *New Ironsides*, but before the February 7, 1864 sinking of the steamer U.S.S. *Housatonic*:

> *...I caused additional means of prevention to be used, as will be seen by copies of enclosed orders, and the Department may be assured that if any of our monitors are injured it will*

*A Confederate "David" on display at the Brooklyn Navy Yard as a war trophy*

*not be for the lack of the utmost vigilance. It is only in smooth water, and when the tide is slack, that any danger is imminent. Last night I went up to the advanced monitor about 9 o'clock. It was an ugly, rainy night, but I found all on the alert. It is indeed dangerous to approach an ironclad, as they fire on the instant. Besides their outriggers and submerged nettings, the water in advance and around is patrolled by several steam tugs and a number of cutters, while the scout boats are thrown out far ahead.*

*If those who so ignorantly or basely endeavor to persuade the public that the monitors here are idle could witness one night of such vigils, they would feel disgraced at having so wantonly traduced the officers and men, who give themselves to such incessant and hard service; a battle would be far preferable.[22]*

The ironclads, especially the monitors as cited by Dahlgren, were not to fall prey to these small vessels and their "torpedoes" of 60 pounds

of black powder. Secretary of the Navy Gideon Wells took considerable heat from the politicians, the press, and public opinion about the apparent idleness of the monitors. It was felt the ironclads should easily crack the nut of Charleston's defenses if only handled properly. Admiral Samuel F. DuPont had tried to force his way into Charleston Harbor in April 1863 while under terrible pressure from the Navy Department, but failed through what was popularly believed to be his inept handling. Although none of the seven monitors engaged were lost in the attack by DuPont, they were all severely pounded by Confederate batteries. The beating was so bad that the captains decided it would be folly to return to the attack the next day. Although correct in his assessment of the monitors' deficient offensive capabilities, Admiral DuPont publicly expressed his doubts, leading to an escalating squabble with the Navy Department and the loss of his job. Admiral Dahlgren knew very well not to follow in DuPont's footsteps or to lose any one of the precious monitors, especially to such a contraption as a Rebel torpedo boat.

The power of the small torpedo boat, submersible or semi-submersible, lay in the confined explosive power of 60 pounds of powder. Again, Daniel Ammen noted in his letter that "It appears that a long heavy pole is used as an outrigger and the torpedo, sunk to a given depth in the water, is brought up against a vessel and six detonating caps make the explosion almost certain...."[23]

By inducing the charge to detonate under about eight feet of water, the weight of the water above the explosion was enough to cause crucial compression against a wood or thin iron plate hull. The resulting destructive compromise of the hull led to the quick demise of the ship. If the charge detonated too close to the surface, as with the October 5, 1863, attack on the U.S.S. New Ironsides, the explosive force surfaced in a magnificent waterfall display, but did little or no damage to the ship's hull. Distance beneath the surface was critical to the destructive force of the torpedo.

The threat to the fleet and the ironclads was very real. Lieutenant Commander Cillery of the monitor U.S.S. *Catskill* gives some insight into an evening on station:

> ...*About 9:40 p.m. observed something low in the water coming toward us on our starboard quarter from seaward. Hailed and, received no reply, fired at it. It sheered off and shortly after approached us on the port quarter; hailed and fired again at it and turned the guns of the turret toward it. It kept off and I sent the picket boat to watch its movements. The boat returned shortly and the officer reported it a torpedo steamer moving toward the* Ironsides. *I immediately made signal 597 and dispatched the picket boat to notify the ironclads. About half an hour afterwards observed firing of musketry in the direction of the ironclads.*
>
> *At quarter past 11 observed what seemed to be the same low object moving close to the shore from Moultrie House to off Fort Moultrie, when it disappeared in the obscurity.*
>
> *During the mid watch, about 2, saw musketry firing in the direction of the* Ironsides, *after which all was quiet.*[24]

Monitors could and did endure hours of hard pounding by the largest guns available to the Confederates. These ironclads, as a class of ship, had been damaged heavily, but never fatally, in firefights with Rebel batteries. Still, none of the ships in the fleet, including these tough ironclads, wanted to face a torpedo charge. Although a Confederate semi-submersible or submersible never sank a monitor class vessel, several monitors did sink with catastrophic loss of life from the effects of moored "torpedoes" exploding under the hull.

## Death of Tecumseh

Perhaps the most significant and unstudied military treasure in the United States is buried in the slime and ooze bottom of Mobile Bay, Alabama. There, in a continual ebb and flow of silt, sand, and modern pollution, lies U.S.S. *Tecumseh*, a Canonicus class monitor. She serves as the tomb for a reported ninety-two officers and men who went to their untimely and rapid deaths within and under her iron plates. The *Tecumseh*, when she met her sudden, violent end, was an improved third generation version of the original U.S.S. *Monitor*. As she rests today, the Tecumseh's massive iron form represents the surviving relic of the Federal Navy's greatest loss of life in a single incident during the Civil War. But, most important, she is a historical treasure trove beyond measure.

The U.S.S. *Tecumseh* is a time capsule of American Naval technology and culture dated precisely to August 5, 1864, the day the ship propelled itself to the bottom during the opening hour of Admiral Farragut's push into Mobile Bay. *Tecumseh* led a line of ironclads preceding the wooden ships into the range of Fort Morgan's gun and the torpedo field. As Commander T. M. Craven passed through the hail of Confederate iron, he ordered *Tecumseh* out of the narrow channel to challenge the oncoming enemy ironclad, the lumbering C.S.S. *Tennessee*. Ordering the ship's helm to port, Commander Craven unknowingly headed *Tecumseh* directly above a large Rebel mine. Within an instant an explosion viciously lifted and rolled the ironclad, ripping a mortal wound in the ship's bottom. With little reserve buoyancy, the combination of the exploded opening in *Tecumseh's* bottom and

*Commander Craven of* Tecumseh.

The *Tecumseh's* keel was laid down in September 1862 and with the various changes ordered it took until the following September to get her launched. Her gun battery was delivered and installed. *Tecumseh* received two 15-inch smoothbores of an improved version over the ones mounted in the Passaic class. The earlier 15-inch guns were too short in barrel length to allow the muzzle of the huge cannon to clear the gun port, which again called for Yankee ingenuity in jury-rigging a solution. Yet another six months would be required to get *Tecumseh* ready. By the last week of March 1864 the ship was safely delivered and under navy control, only to be hauled out of the water to have the bottom scraped and painted. The *Tecumseh* had become so fouled since launching that making six knots in still water was difficult, if not impossible. It was not until April 19 that *Tecumseh* was commissioned into the U. S. Navy.

With the last of her problems settled, Commander Craven headed his command south to serve under the timid Admiral Samuel F. Lee and his squadron based at Hampton Roads, Vir-

her attack speed rapidly filled the ship. She started her death's dive, going down by the bow and healing to port. Choking black smoke billowed from her stack to mark her two minute agony. Desperate men in the turret scrambled out the gun ports. Below, others clawed through the darkness, fighting the rush of cold water, cursing their plight and praying for salvation in their last breath.

In her final moments, *Tecumseh's* stern burst from the water exposing her massive propeller. She shuddered, rolled, then finally sucked the water's surface, vacuuming those sailors still within reach. In the Rebel fortifications and aboard the closing Confederate fleet, men cheered as *Tecumseh* was sent to her death.

For the Federals, the battle continued. Cool heads settled the brief confusion and continued the fight. There was no time for reflection or remorse; vengeance would come in a fight to the finish.

U.S.S. *Tecumseh* had a short career, mainly distinguished by her death in the fight at Mobile Bay. From her commission in April 1864, her total service was less than four months. Much more time was spent in her construction, modifications, and getting her accepted into the navy.

*Paymaster George Work, drowned on* Tecumseh.

ginia. *Tecumseh* was part of an iron curtain on the lower James River, a shield for the operations of Generals Butler and Grant. Three Canonicus monitors, *Tecumseh*, *Canonicus*, and *Saugus*, served along with the double turreted monitor, *Onondaga*, and the captured Confederate ironclad, C.S.S. *Atlanta*. The *Atlanta*, surrendering after being torn open by 15 inch shots from the U.S.S. *Weehawken*, was now repaired and ready to face the threat now assembled on the James River below Richmond. Apart from some potshots from the river banks and a long range cannon duel, *Tecumseh's* baptism by fire was not particularly glorious.

Although General Butler succeeded in getting his army bottled up, General Grant commenced the massive bloodletting that would eventually drain the proud Army of Northern Virginia of its last drop of resolve. By July 5, *Tecumseh* sailed south, with orders to go first to Pensacola, then on to Mobile Bay and immortality.

The story of U.S.S. *Tecumseh* is more than her short and relatively lackluster life in the United States Navy. She is a pearl of mud encrusted iron, waiting for rediscovery. Although there have been several attempts to salvage the ship, thankfully none have succeeded. She is too valuable for amateur plunder, government blundering or continued historical neglect. Recent explorations of the ship have uncovered attempts by unknown divers to plunder her remains. Serious people, however, are doing significant work to determine if she can ever be resurrected from her present crypt of mud. Preservation and interpretation are vital to study how this ship fits into our knowledge of the war and her demise. Currently there is little or no funding for these efforts. The fate of *Tecumseh* is questionable at best.

The death of *Tecumseh* and her crew has been generally overlooked in the history of the Civil War, overshadowed by Admiral Farragut's success in closing Mobile Bay as a Confederate port. In so doing, the Admiral gloriously ran past the Confederate forts and mine field ("Damn the torpedoes...") and delivered a crushing one-sided victory over the lame C.S.S. *Tennessee* and her likewise feeble naval consorts.

The price of victory is not always a point of discussion. Attention is lavished on the glory of victory, not its price. At best *Tecumseh's* death gets only passing mention in any recounting of the Battle of Mobile Bay, and little notice in the overall story of the war. Though her death seems to garner little respect, it may be just that lack of attention that has saved the ship. How much time is left to properly study and save the remains of U.S.S. *Tecumseh* from the ravages of nature and modern day pirates, is unknown.

# Total Failure

The monitors pictured here are U.S.S. *Shawnee* and U.S.S. *Wassuc*. Both ships are of the failed Casco, also called the Yazoo, class shallow draft monitor design. Neither vessel saw active war service and, as pictured, represent little more than a rusting reminder of the dreadful waste of money that the entire class embodied. Before construction of this class of monitors, the taxpayers of the United States had not suffered such waste.

Within this class of monitors were 20 ships, and 20 failures. Each vessel cost nearly $500,000 each; over ten million dollars were spent on a worthless project. Perhaps the most stupefying aspect of this boondoggle was that not one man lost a job as a result. Probably little was made of the failures because the construction contracts were spread around by the government to twelve separate cities beginning as early as September 9, 1863. This continued as a building project until the ships were launched in 1865. Since the work was nationally well dispersed, Northern industrialists and workers enjoyed the boom of shipbuilding and job security. By the time the first ships slid down the building ways, national focus was directed elsewhere: celebration of the war's end, the assassination of the president, retribution, the Indian territory, and connecting the nation by rail.

The early concept for the class was brought before John Ericsson in an effort to enlist his aid with the project. However, he was busy with contracts on several other monitors of his own design. Responsibility to become involved in yet another project was beyond even the fabled endurance of John Ericsson. Although he completed some initial drawings:

*...Ericsson was not able to give time to the details of the final design, which was entrusted to Chief Engineer Alban Stimers, U.S. Navy, who became the Chief Inspector of Ironclads and head of the light-draft monitor project."*[25]

Casco class monitors were designed to be light draft for service on the Mississippi River and coastal waters. They allowed deeper penetration of shallow Southern waterways by an ironclad with enough armor and armament to defeat anything the Rebels had upriver, any fortification or battery awaiting Federal movement. Initial specifications requested a ship drawing but four feet of water. The question of how to do it was presented to Ericsson, who promptly pronounced the concept impossible. He completed some rough design and engineering drawings, but the real project was then turned over to Chief Engineer Albert Stimers, who would develop and execute plans for a class of monitors drawing six feet of water. Since Ericsson had dismissed Stimers and his pet project, they remained with little in common beyond their massive egos. The stage was set for the comedy of errors to follow. When Assis-

tant Secretary of the Navy Fox later wrote Ericsson for his opinion of Stimers's plans, the odd genius Ericsson found little to his liking and, "refused to take responsibility for the light draft monitors"[26]

Naturally, Stimers was out to prove his worth by employing his skills to outdo Ericsson. Assigned to the monitor bureau in New York, he succeeded in taking control of its day to day functions away from its nominal head, Admiral Francis Gregory:

*In charge of the "monitor bureau" as general superintendent of ironclads was the aged, infirmed Rear Admiral Francis H. Gregory. Seventy-three years of age in 1861, the old line officer, who had served in the navy since 1809, had been brought out of retirement, given increased rank, and set at the desk in the New York office to administer the steam and ironclad building program. As the general inspector of ironclads (also known as the general inspector of steam machinery for the Navy), the department assigned Chief Engineer Alban C. Stimers, a vain, clever, and immensely ambitious naval engineer, who had distinguished himself by*

*U.S.S.* Shawnee *and U.S.S.* Wassuc, *Charlestown (Boston) Navy Yard. Awaiting their ultimate fate as iron scrap.*

*supervising the construction of the* Monitor *and then serving on that vessel throughout the battle of Hampton Roads.*[27]

Stimers would not let the project slip through his fingers just because Ericsson did not bestow his blessing. With the opportunities presented to Stimers by his association and proximity to the offices of Admiral Gregory,

*...Stimers soon had a combined engineering and construction bureau of his own in operation, staffed with engineers, draftsmen, and clerks whose numbers almost equaled in size the entire force of all the navy bureaus combined. Intoxicated by the importance of his work and impatient with red tape and supervision, Stimers largely ignored the bureaus in Washington, paid mere lip service to his administrative superior, Admiral Gregory, and freely went on his way in designing the monitors.*[28]

However, the Casco class was not only plagued by an egotistical genius but also by engineers who with every battle report tried to

*Alban Stimers, dismissed by Ericsson, pressed ahead with the Casco class monitors.*

improve upon the final design by insisting on multiple changes as the ships were under construction. In effect, this created a cut-and-paste monitor,

*...constructed on four or five different plans, and no two plans corresponded with each other in any particular, form or specification. The officers in charge of those vessels didn't know from day to day what plan they should adopt; they were waiting the development of some battle before some southern fort, or some order from the Bureau at Washington; and when those battles were fought every engineer suggested something in regard to the vessels, and there were changes from the commencement to the end. Hardly a week elapsed during the construction of these vessels that we didn't have a change of great importance, sometimes adding thousands of dollars to the vessel and delaying completion of it.*

*It was impossible to complete the vessels within the contract time on account of so many changes and delays in the plans. We didn't receive plans for sometimes eighteen months.*[29]

Because Stimers succeeded in alienating Ericsson and other influential navy departments and officers of superior rank, he received little help on the project. In the end, the design, management and execution of the work clearly showed that Stimers was never equal to the task. The final ships were so faulty that they were universally condemned as categorical failures upon the launching of the first ship of the class, U.S.S. *Chimo*. When she entered the water, the new light draft monitor's deck was nearly awash. In this condition without turret, guns, coal, stores, and men, the ship would be submerged when complete. The sensational failure of design set off a firestorm in Washington. In Secretary of the Navy Gideon Wells' diary, he commented on the light draft monitors: "...I found serious difficulties existed, requiring essential modifications and a large increase in expenditure to make the vessels efficient or capable of flotation with their armament."[30] The failure of the Casco class so vexed Wells that he further wrote, "...I look upon the whole transaction as the most unfortunate that has taken place during my administration of the Navy Department.[31]

The first five ships were launched, then promptly converted from failed monitors into failed torpedo and gun boats. These ships were fitted with the Wood-Lay spar-torpedo gear and mounted an unprotected 11-inch gun on the open deck. The astounding lack of protection for the gun crew made any possibility of a fight questionable, especially on rivers narrow enough to make enemy rifle fire, as well as field artillery, deadly effective. Additionally, the spar torpedo came into question as an effective weapon when the maximum speed reached by the converted monitors barely reached five miles an hour. Men assigned to command and crew these first five ships were well aware that they served aboard the most expensive junk in the Civil War navy.

The other fifteen ships of the class were rebuilt on the building ways, adding additional depth to the deck, thereby killing any pretense of being light draft and adding from $55,000 to $115,000 each to the cost of the remaining ships. However, none of the fifteen were completed in time to play even a minor scene in the closing days of the war.

Regarding the failed Casco class, the following article concerns the actual launching of one of the ships. There is a "Keystone Cops" air surrounding the launching, if the account can be fully believed. What needs to be remembered is that when this ship was launched, it was essentially scrap. It had no purpose; the war was over, and it had nothing to do but to await completion at the fitting out pier. Then several years later, it suffered the breakers turning her plates of iron into scrap for potbelly stoves and the like. During the launching of U.S.S. *Umpqua* on December 21, 1865, into the Monongahela River at Pittsburgh, Pa., the river was at flood stage and moving at 8 miles an hour—not good conditions for an iron ship:

> *Her stern was submerged over forty feet (in launching) and a huge swell washed part of her deck, which in a few minutes was a glare of ice. It was expected that on entering the water, the* Umpqua *would plunge across to the Pittsburgh side of the river, where the* Albion *waited for her. During other launches, the current had been out of the Allegheny, the Monongahela being a pool of back water. This time, however, there were sixteen feet of water in the Monongahela, and a current of eight miles an hour. When the current struck the stern of the ship, she commenced an astonishing series of gyrations,*

*A perfect picture of failure. The U.S.S.* Casco, *unable to float her turret and guns, was turned into a gunboat of even more questionable worth.*

*ran into the coal tug* Whale, *broke her guards forward and some of her stanchions, and nearly sank some of her tow. At another swing she sank a barge belonging to the Alps Coal Company, and struck the coal tug* Alps *with such force as to break part of her guards and careen her over on one side, until it was feared that she would turn over. Steamers* Albion *and* Brilliant *meanwhile danced about her, making futile efforts to check her wild career. Several times these steamboats were nearly run down and crushed by the weighty vessel.*[32]

Following the near disaster, *Umpqua* was ultimately secured to her fitting-out pier and completed in September of the following year; her total cost amounted to $595,652.36. She remained, rusting, in the navy for nine years, and was finally sold at auction on September 12, 1874, at New Orleans for $8,900.

## A Bogus View

One of many photographers with a series of images to sell after the Civil War, John C. Taylor of Hartford, Connecticut, sold a unique view of a Civil War ironclad monitor. On the reverse of the card it reads as follows:

> *The "Monitor" showing her ports open, and the muzzles of her "barkers." This view also shows dents in the turret, where she was struck by Rebel shot, but this side of the turret does not show as many marks of shot as No. 111.*
>
> *These are the original views taken by the Government Artists, during 1861-2-3-4-5. They can be obtained only of John C. Taylor, 17 Allen Place, Hartford, Conn.*

This, of course, is not the famous U.S.S. *Monitor*. There are several obvious things wrong with the view, which suggests that the ship so pictured is not the ship referred to on the reverse. The base ring around the turret is the first giveaway; the second is the large muzzle of a 15-inch smoothbore gun. Neither item saw service on the original ship. The base rings first appeared as retrofit items after the turrets of

the monitors were being jammed by Rebel fire. A solid shot would hit the deck close to the turret and either start or warp the deck plate. This, in turn, prevented the turret from rotating by jamming the turret as it tried to rotate. The base rings, manufactured in sections of brass, were bolted through the turret. In this way the brass would take the concussion of the striking shot and not allow the deck plates to be struck, thereby possibly jamming the turret. As

*The unaltered view.*
*Now you see it...*

*The bogus view.*
*Now you don't!*

for the 15-inch gun, *Monitor* never had one. She was armed with two 11-inch smoothbore Dahlgren guns, and the muzzles cleared the gunports, much in the same way the 11-inch gun does in this view. Due to poor planning and manufacturing problems with the 15-inch guns, the muzzle was too large to be run out of the gun port and thus had to be fired within the turret proper. That also was a dead giveaway as to the class of monitor involved. So, with the base ring, and the two different size guns, with one inside the turret, the picture clearly shows this ship to be one of the 10 Passaic class monitors, except for one very important thing. This view does not show the pilothouse atop the turret as was the case in the Passaics. The photo is a FAKE!

The art of photography was still new in the period these views were taken and later sold. The Civil War was a hot seller and as part of anyone's collection, one would want a representation of *Monitor*, the ship that saved the navy! If the view was not available, it was not too difficult to make another view fit the bill. The technical process to "massage" an image, and make something new out of another view was well within the knowledge of most competent photographers. It made good business sense to give the public what they wanted. There is no way to know if the manipulation of the image was done by Taylor, or if the image had been "doctored" when the Connecticut Yankee came into possession of the negative, then proceeded to produce and sell the resulting photograph. Whoever made this image knew enough about the ships to recognize that the pilothouse had to disappear from atop the turret to make the image appear to be *Monitor* to the uneducated buyer.

The real image, shown below the Taylor view, reveals the ship as it should appear. The ship is reported to be U.S.S. *Passaic* in the waters outside Charleston, S.C. The dents are compliments of the Confederate States from hundreds of guns concentrated within the strategic area of the harbor and its defenses.

Speculation over the image could go on and on, but today it is a unique photo. It presents a special view of a ship that never existed, done in the best of Yankee intentions and motives—profit.

# USS Onondaga

Named for a lake in upstate New York, this unique monitor spent her short naval career on the James River in Virginia. Very powerful, she was one of a kind, a class of one with no other vessel built to her specifications. Her purpose was to deny the James River to the powerful Confederate naval forces above Drewery's Bluff.

The Confederate forces had three powerful ironclads operating on the James below Richmond, C.S.S. *Richmond*, C.S.S. *Virginia II*, and C.S.S. *Fredericksburg*. All three ships were of the Porter design, perfected by the Rebel navy. Any one was individually capable of destroying the wooden fleet of merchant ships fueling the Army of the Potomac. Even swift and heavily armed Union gunboats were no match for these Rebel ironclads in the narrow, twisting, James River.

Under General Grant, the Army of the Potomac had become a machine grinding away endlessly at the Rebel army under the brilliant Robert E. Lee, slowly turning that army into dust. But Grant's army and his campaign depended entirely on the U.S. Navy for its life in the field. The Union effort was supplied and sustained over the water, for nothing could be transported overland.

As the heat was turned up by Grant in the spring 1864 campaign, the almost ceaseless murder finally brought the opposing armies to a siege situation before Petersburg. President Lincoln paid a field visit to the army in July 1864, and went aboard U.S.S. *Onondaga* in the first week of July to inspect this proud ship. A third assistant engineer aboard *Onondaga* witnessed the event and in a letter home commented:

*The President, Generals Grant and Butler, and other distinguished officials paid us a visit last week. "Old Abe" got off two or three good jokes while on board. He appeared to be quite pleased with his visit.*[33]

These men knew that the success of the campaign and daily operations of the Army of the Potomac singularly depended on the success of the navy in supplying the army's demands in material and men. The unique vessel in this lifeline was U.S.S. *Onondaga*. There was no

*The U.S.S.* Onondaga *on the James River.*

ship more powerful on the river, and nothing to match her guns. General U. S. Grant felt so strongly about protection for his base of operations that he expected the navy to sacrifice its ships before giving way to any Confederate attack. He said as much in his communication to Navy Secretary Gideon Wells on January 24, 1865: "It would be better to obstruct the channel of the river with sunken gunboats than that a rebel ram should reach City Point."[34]

Confederates were well aware of the union seaborne lifeline. At the urging of General Robert E. Lee, plans were made to send out the Rebel fleet to take on the union ironclad, and destroy the heart of the Union Army's base of operations at City Point. This strike led directly to the court martial of the captain of the *Onondaga* for his actions on the night of the Rebel attack.

The U.S.S. *Onondaga* was built under contract with G.W. Quintard of New York, N.Y. She displaced 1,250 tons and her two turrets were armed each with a 15-inch smoothbore Dahlgren and a 150-pdr. Parrott rifle. Commissioned at the New York Navy Yard on March 24, 1864, she departed for the war in early April, and arrived about the 23rd, ready for duty as part of the North Atlantic Blockading Squadron under Admiral Samuel P. Lee. Her commanding officer was Capt. William A. Parker, a veteran of the navy since 1832 when he first went to sea at age sixteen. When the Rebel attack came on the night of January 24-25, the Union Navy was waiting, but not fully ready, despite being informed of the pending attack by several Rebel deserters. This intelligence set off the flurry of telegraphs from General U.S. Grant, calling for the return of the other ironclads from North Carolina. Grant was worried about his lifeline, and rightfully so as the attack developed.

When the attack came, the Rebel ram *Fredericksburg* succeeded in passing the obstructions in the waters. It was forced to halt as the other two ironclads, C.S.S. *Virginia II* and

C.S.S. *Richmond* grounded in the night before reaching the breach in the Union obstructions. Captain Parker of *Onondaga* did not engage the oncoming Rebel ships, thinking it prudent to fall back and await assistance with the dawn. Union shore batteries poured steady fire into the Rebel ironclads as *Onondaga* awaited the coming light. With the dawn, *Onondaga* steamed back upriver to face the Rebel rams. She came about presented herself broadside to the Rebel ships and opened fire with her four guns. The Rebels, having lost the element of surprise, retreated back up the river under the safety of the Confederate batteries at Drewery's Bluffs. The Rebel ships had been roughly handled by the Union gunners; C.S.S. *Virginia* was struck well over 75 times and quite cut up, although not put out of combat.

For his part in the action, or lack of it, Captain Parker was relieved of his command at the "request" of General U.S. Grant through the Secretary of the Navy. Gideon Wells wasted no time in getting Parker off *Onondaga* and away from the action.

A court of inquiry found Captain Parker guilty of the two charges brought against him and he was sentenced to be dismissed from the Navy of the United States. Upon review of the proceedings, all was dismissed by Gideon Wells who stated that the proceedings and conclusions of the Court "...somewhat embarrassed the Department." And further, "...All the allegations in the specifications, against which the accused was warned to defend himself, are either disproved or are insufficient to prove guilt...."[35] Captain Parker was relieved from arrest and returned to service, but his career had received a damning blow from which it would never recover.

Captain Parker was moved to the retired list on December 23, 1865, and assigned to command the receiving ship *Independence* on the California Station from 1866 to 1869. In April 1869, he was promoted to Captain on the retired list and assigned to be lighthouse inspector for the coast of the Gulf of Mexico. This kept him in the service, but far enough away from the men who saw his duty that night fail the standards of his rank, command and responsibility.

As for U.S.S. *Onondaga*, she was, by an Act of Congress, sold back to her builders at government cost, $760,000. This sweetheart deal al-lowed the builders to sell her again, but this time to the French Navy. The French realized the value of a powerful turreted ship of the monitor design long before the British, who stuck exclusively with the broadside ironclad until 1873 when H.M.S. *Devastation* was commissioned into service. The *Onondaga* remained with the French Navy under her original name as a coastal defense ship, was refurbished and regunned several times, then sold for scrap in 1904.

The U.S.S. *Onondaga* was a powerful ship with a short and checkered career. She realized a visit from President Lincoln, had her commander court martialed, and finally, became the object of naval affection and greed in the deal to sell her into the French Navy.

# The Cock of the Weehawken

*Another life was lost, which the "dignity of history" has not deigned to notice. The crew of the* Weehawken *had a pet. (What man-of-war's crew has not?) It was a noble chanticleer, who felt as much at home on the ironclad as in his own native barnyard. He had many "taking ways," and had done many things that his proud ship-mates loved to tell of. When the* Atlanta *was captured, and Captain Webb came aboard the* Weehawken *to give up his sword, Chapman strutted to the ship's side, and "took a look" at the captain, then he mounted the pilot-house, flapped his wings, and crowed lustily three times; giving the honors of war" on behalf of the United States, to the distinguished prisoner. When the* Weehawken *got aground one day, near Fort Sumter, and lay with her hull badly exposed, shelled by the Confederates, and in desperate peril of destruction, Chapman paced the deck in pensive silence for four hours. But as soon as she had been got off, without loss, he mounted the pilot-house and poured from his melodious breast a song of thanksgiving and joy, which was reechoed from the walls of Sumter. Never did he hear the crew "'piped' to quarters," but his voice..."Rose like a anthem rich and strong," to second the call. After having thus "braved the battle and the breeze" during the whole cruise, this noble fowl was "sucked down" with the* Weehawken, *and perished miserably with the ship of which he was the pride and boast. "If he had been killed in one of those long bombardments," said one "old salt," who had survived him, "I shouldn't have felt so bad. That's what we all expect. But to see him fluttering on the waves and going down like a mere land-lubber; it's too much for me to think of." Then lifting his sleeve to wipe the similitude of a tear from his starboard cheek, he added, "I tell you, Judge Cowley, on the word of a man, I'd rather 'a' lost half my prize money than have lost the cock of the old Weehawken."[36]*

Perhaps a sad tale, but it illustrates a danger that all monitors lived with, each and every day. The death of the proud rooster, and about a third of the crew, was visited upon U.S.S. *Weehawken* as she lay at anchor just outside Charleston Harbor. The Passaic class monitor was riding out some rough weather coming out of the east by north, but the sea had seemed to be no threat to the ship.

Monitor class ships were by design extremely low in the water. Most of the coastal monitors of the Ericsson design were only eighteen inches above water at the bow and twelve inches at the stern. The closeness of the deck to the water, and the slight difference between the bow and stern served two similar but different purposes. First, it made the ship less prone to hits from enemy fire. Unlike a broadside man-of-war, a monitor's freeboard, the distance between the water and the deck, was too small to offer a good target to an enemy gunner. Enemy gunners had to aim for a 20-foot turret rather than a long hull, making monitors hard to hit. The second reason for the bow being higher was to keep the ship in such a position as to allow the natural pull of gravity on any water leaking into the ship, at any point, to be directed aft. In the stern were located large, powerful bilge pumps that vacuumed the bilge water and discharged it overboard. However, the critical part of the equation was to keep the bow higher than the stern, never even or lower.

*The Cock of the Old Weehawken.*

There were no pumps forward to pull any water out of the ship that collected forward if the ship was "out of trim."

The *Weehawken* had just replenished her ammunition and the ship was not trimmed properly. There were too many huge shots forward of the ship's center. Though not critical, it added to the elements of fate that combined to sink the ship. A forward hatch had remained open and sea water accumulated forward. This started to bring the ship down by its bow, taking away the critical trim that needed to be maintained. More water entered the ship than buckets could handle and the pumps, in the stern, were rendered ineffective, for there was no way to get the water astern. The outcome was a certainty. The sinking was described in the log of U.S.S. *Montauk*, not too distant from the stricken ironclad:

> *At 2:25 saw the* Weehawken *make signal to flagship and at the same time saw steam escaping from the smokestack, and in a few minutes saw that she was settling fast by the head...At 2:40 she made a heavy roll to starboard, then righted and sank immediately.[37]*

Steam from the smokestack told the death story of the sea water inside the ship. It had risen high enough to attack the boilers and fire box, putting the ship out of power to move or to operate the pumps.

Coastal monitors were precarious as far as the amount of water any one could take on and sustain before the ship was in a sinking condition. Essentially, if any of the Ericsson coastal monitors took on more than 18 inches of water, the entire deck of the ship would be below the water line. Monitors were not designed to be submersibles.

No doubt there were mistakes made that fateful day, December 6, 1863. But none suspected that the errors would compound into tragedy for *Weehawken*. With too much water and the ship not properly trimmed, she sank quickly, taking down men, boys, and the unlucky rooster. John Ericsson's assessment of the sinking was offered:

*I have very closely examined Assistant Inspector Hughes, who witnessed the sinking of the* Weehawken, *and who conversed with her pilot and several of her crew, and I have no hesitation in asserting that the water which entered through the forward hatch until the vessel was too much by the head to render the pumps of any avail, and after the fatal condition through the hawse hole, caused the sinking of the ironclad.*[38]

Following the sinking, personal accounts and boards of inquiries filled the records and account for the demise of the monitor. Plans were offered to raise her; divers were sent into 30 feet of water to inspect the ship as she lay on the muddy bottom. But the most pressing issue was the continuation of the war, their immediate concern, cracking the tough nut that Charleston presented to the Federal government. Orders issued to other monitor commanders directed them to avoid a similar fate. John Ericsson offered some additional engineering partial fixes, and the war went on.

# John Wilkes Booth

With the final, dying breath hissing out of his lungs, John Wilkes Booth mournfully sighed, "Useless...useless." Just several weeks before Booth's death on April 26, 1865, the Civil War was ending. Military engagements of any consequence were over, and the U.S. Navy brought in the warships that were no longer needed. One, U.S.S. *Montauk*, a Passaic class monitor, had many months of hard service to her credit. The veteran ironclad, crewless, rusted peacefully in the Washington Navy Yard as she awaited her disposition.

President Abraham Lincoln, to escape daily pressures, often rode to the navy yard where he sat on the ships' decks. On board *Montauk*, Lincoln enjoyed a peace and solitude not possible in the war bloated city of Washington. For short periods, he could escape its multitude of politicians, generals and underlings, office seekers, pretenders and every other description of humankind that takes roost in war capitals. Although the war was still active in several locations, the recent surrender of Robert E. Lee's Army of Northern Virginia lifted a huge weight from his shoulders. That once fearsome specter of secession was but a memory. The world seemed a better place for President Lincoln and his wife as they sat quietly and enjoyed the setting sun from the deck of *Montauk*.

Within weeks, the president was dead at the hand of John Wilkes Booth. The *Montauk* became the prison for one of the conspirators and the morgue for the body of his assassin. The deck served as the theater for the autopsy of Booth, upon a stage most recently used as a carpenter's bench. Along with *Montauk*, U.S.S. *Saugus* served as a temporary prison.

With the murder of President Lincoln, the largest manhunt in America ensued as the whole nation was thrown into spasms of revenge. The chase cumulated in the capture of David Herold and the death of John Wilkes Booth outside Port Royal, Virginia. Both men were cornered in a tobacco barn where David Herold quickly surrendered. Booth, however, decided to remain inside the rickety structure. The barn was put quickly to the torch to flush out the despised assassin.

In the confusion of gunfire, flames and smoke, Booth was shot in the neck, then dragged from the inferno, mortally wounded by Sgt. Boston Corbett of New York. Corbett, a veteran horse soldier, bible thumping Christian convert, was but recently exchanged after five months' imprisonment in Andersonville Prison. Laid out on the porch of a nearby house, Booth's curtain call took about two and a half hours before he breathed his last, at just about dawn. In his diary, Booth had recently penned: "I am here in despair...I have too great a soul to die like a criminal. Oh! May He spare me that and let me die bravely."[39]

The fatal shooting of Booth was against orders to return Booth alive, issued by the *de facto* President, Secretary of War Stanton. Yet Sergeant Corbett became an instant celebrity. The slaying of Booth by a religiously fervent soul signaled the end of the Civil War, just as the first blood drawn by John Brown had signaled the beginning.

David Herold and Booth's stiffening body were loaded upon the steamer *John S. Ide*, then transported to Alexandria and on to the Washington Navy Yard by tug for final disposition. After transfer of Booth's body to the ironclad *Montauk*, identification of the battered and bloated remains was made by no less than ten individuals. As Booth's corpse lay upon a carpenter's bench on deck, under a canvas awning, an autopsy was performed by Surgeon General Dr. Joseph Barnes. This was reported in the May 13, 1865, edition of *Harper's Weekly* as follows:

> *A post-mortem examination of the remains took place on board the Monitor* Montauk *before his burial. BOOTH'S body was laid out on a carpenter's bench between the stern and turret, wrapped in a gray blanket, and a guard placed over it. The lips of the corpse were tightly compressed, and the blood had settled in the lower part of the face and neck. Otherwise his face was pale, and wore a wild, haggard look, indicating exposure to the elements and a rough time generally in his skulking fight. His hair was disarranged and dirty, and apparently had not been combed since he took his flight. The head and breast were alone exposed to view, the lower portion of the body, including the hands and feet, being covered with a tarpaulin. The shot which terminated his life entered on the left side, at the back of the neck, a point not far distant from that in which his victim, our lamented President, was shot.*
>
> *On the night of the 27th of April a small row boat received the remains of the murderer, and no one save two men, it is said, know the place or manner of his sepulture.*[40]

Word rapidly spread to the excited city of Washington that Booth's body was at the Navy Yard. Secretary of War Stanton ordered the immediate removal of Booth's body, and burial in a secret place. General Lafayette Baker, chief of the department's Secret Service, was charged with the duty. The rotting corpse was removed from *Montauk* to a small rowboat and taken down the Anacostia River to the Arsenal grounds for secret burial in the Old Penitentiary. Booth's mortal remains, sewed up in a tarpaulin, were buried in an ammunition case under the stone flooring of the old prison's dining hall. His body, a few years later, was released quietly to his family, the boxed remains removed to Baltimore for reburial.

Below decks, U.S.S. *Montauk* housed coconspirator David Herold. As with all the prisoners, he was placed in hand and leg irons by his jailers. Even Herold's senses were denied him in his prison—his eyes were covered with cotton wadding and his head was encased in a heavy

*John Wilkes Booth*

cotton hood. A small, roughly cut hole allowed labored breathing in the cold, damp interior of the ironclad, and provided a means for eating and drinking. Herold and the others, convicted by a kangaroo court, met their collective fate at the end of the hangman's noose a few months later, still hooded on a sweltering July afternoon.

The U.S.S. *Montauk* remained in the Navy for another thirty nine years. She would never again witness anyone so grand as President Lincoln or anything so dramatic as the Booth autopsy

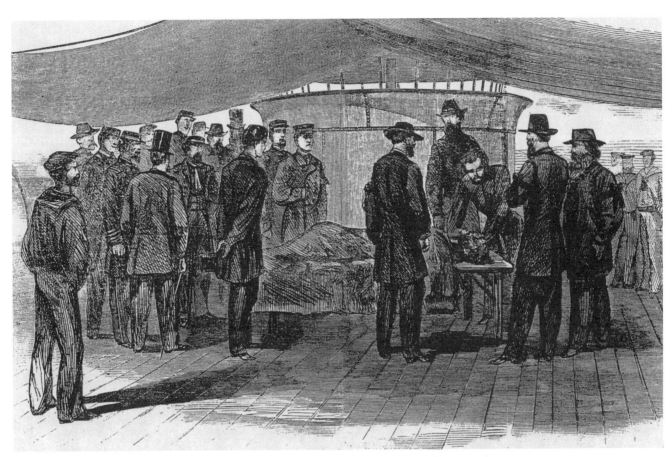

*Post mortem of John Wilkes Booth on board the monitor* Montauk.

*In this post war view showing five monitors at the Washington Navy Yard, the U.S.S.* Montauk *is the 2nd ship from the right.*

# PHOTO GALLERY

**Officers of U.S.S. Sangamon**

*This Passaic class monitor was a fixture on the James River where this image was recorded.  Sangamon was part of the ironclad insurance policy demanded by General Grant.  After crossing the James, Grant established his base of supply at City Point, Virginia, for the final operations against General Lee's still lethal army.  This is an interesting image which includes, beyond the officers, the bullet shield atop the turret, the ship's bell rigged on the turret's side and the brass Dahlgren gun secured to the deck.*

### U.S.S. Miantonomoh

*At the end of her career, the U.S.S.* Miantonomoh, *the first monitor to cross the Atlantic Ocean, lies in the still waters of the Charlestown (Boston) Navy Yard. The ship is totally housed-over in a sheathing of wood to protect her iron decks and upper works from the ravages of weather.*

### Monadnock *and* Camanche

*An interesting postwar view indicating the fate of the monitors, some sooner than later, as in this case. The large double-turret monitor may very well be the U.S.S.* Monadnock *as she is in the process of being broken up in the Mare Island Navy Yard in San Francisco Bay, 1874. At this point the ship has already been lightened by the removal of her turrets, guns and side armor, and she is but so much scrap waiting to be melted down and recast into thousands of other items made of iron.*

*Barely visible out in the harbor is another single turret monitor of the Passaic class, most likely the U.S.S.* Camanche, *the only other monitor in San Francisco Bay. Camanche would survive in various roles, including a training ship, until she too was sold for scrap in 1899.*

## Monitors under construction

*An amazing, previously unpublished image of the U.S.S. Passaic and the U.S.S. Montauk on the building ways at the Continental Yard at Green Point shipyard, New York. Passaic (in the ship house) is the lead ship of the new and improved monitor class to follow the original U.S.S. Monitor. She would be launched August 30, 1862.*

*The U.S.S. Montauk, with incomplete hull side armor, would follow Passaic into the water several months later with her launching on October 9, 1862. Command of this ship would be given to John Worden, the wounded captain of the original U.S.S. Monitor.*

***U.S.S. Canonicus** and **U.S.S. Sangamon***

*In the spring of 1865, these two monitors, the Canonicus class monitor upstream and Passaic class monitor below stand guard on the James River. In the foreground is what appears to be a 9-inch gun awaiting target practice on any Confederate vessel foolish enough to steam into the area.*

***Coaling on station***

*The U.S.S. Canonicus takes on coal from a lighter while on station in the James River. On the after section of the monitor's deck is rigged a large awning to provide some relief from the sun. Smoke is plainly visible from the galley pipe just aft of the turret, indicating the preparation of a meal to be served shortly to the hardworking men.*

### *Forever remembered*

*A young U.S. Army private, Charles Dickinson, sketched his impression of the Navy off Seabrook Island, South Carolina in 1863. In the first sketch (above), he provides his portrait of the U.S.S. Weehawken. The monitor* Weehawken *was famous for her capture of the Rebel ironclad C.S.S. Atlanta in June 1863.* Weehawken *would meet a tragic fate, sinking from poor ship-keeping while on station outside Charleston. The second view (below) includes at least four monitors of the Passaic class, as well as several other ships of war and supply.*

*Asst. Surgeon Daniel McMutrie*
*U.S.S.* Sangamon

*Surgeon Francis Weld*
*U.S.S.* Nantucket

### Cleaning up the mess

*Duty aboard the monitors exhausted the crews in short order and it was the men of the medical service who attempted to stem the ever rising tide of sickness and debility. Combat and accidental casualties were always part of a surgeon's call. But the monitors were especially harsh because of the extreme heat and almost nonexistent ventilation. Because of the poor conditions, crewmen rarely lasted a full enlistment aboard a monitor.*

### Lucky DeLuce—wounded in action

*Acting Ensign Theodore F. DeLuce was serving aboard monitor U.S.S.* Montauk *in Charleston Harbor as commander of* Montauk's *15-inch gun.* Montauk *was engaged in a night action against Fort Sumter on August 23, 1864.* Montauk *"...was hit heavily six times on the turret, side armor, and decks. Acting Ensign Theo. F. DeLuce was slightly wounded in the left arm by a flying bolt head while in the turret."*

*The turrets were constructed with layers of iron plates, held together by long bolts running through all plates. The interior of a monitor's turret could become a lethal place when the enemy's solid shot struck and drove in bolt heads, nuts and other slivers of iron. DeLuce was lucky.*

### *Prelude to the day that changed naval warfare*

*William P. Randall and William Kennison were serving as shipmates aboard the U.S.S.* Cumberland *when a naval nightmare, the C.S.S.* Virginia, *attacked. It was March 7 and* Virginia *was intent on the destruction of the U.S. Naval presence at Hampton Roads, Virginia. These two men were determined to make the ironclad pay a price for its venture.*

*Randall was a New Bedford whaling captain who joined the war effort early. On that fateful day he was in charge of* Cumberland's *aft pivot gun and continued to fight as the ship sank. His gun was the last to fire at the Southern ironclad as* Cumberland's *gun deck slipped below the water.*

*Fighting his ship like a demon possessed, Kennison's personal accounting for that day exceeded all expectations for a young volunteer officer. Not long after the engagement, he was cited and promoted to acting volunteer lieutenant for gallant and meritorious conduct.*

*After the day's fight was completed, U.S.S.* Cumberland *and U.S.S.* Congress *were destroyed, victims of the Confederate ironclad. That evening the U.S.S.* Monitor *arrived at Hampton Roads and tied up alongside the grounded U.S.S.* Minnesota. *Aboard the helpless warship, Moses S. Stuyvesant nursed his wound suffered as a result of a shell fired from the* Virginia *at extreme range. Moses worried for his ship, which he will one day command, and wondered if the little ironclad alongside could meet and match the Rebel ship. The next day, March 8, 1862, would witness the first naval engagement between ironclads.*

*William P. Randall*

*Moses S. Stuyvesant*

*William W. Kennison*

### Some popular views

*These four lithograph cdv's afforded the public with visual awareness and reporting of their ironclad navy in action.*

*View 1 shows the assault of the U.S.S. Monitor and her consorts on the Confederate defenses below Richmond. The U.S. Navy had hoped to enter Richmond through the back door of the James River after the Confederates destroyed C.S.S. Virginia. The Rebel Fort Darling, situated high above the river, drove off the attackers with well aimed shots. It was an early demonstration of the need for combined operations to successfully take a land fortification.*

*View 2 shows the U.S.S. Passaic in battle trim, the proud lead ship of the Passaic class. She is the first of ten new monitors built after the original U.S.S. Monitor that are launched to crush the rebellion.*

*View 3 shows the Milwaukee Class monitor U.S.S. Chickasaw. This class was designed and built by James Eads of Mississippi River fame. Chickasaw was instrumental in bringing about the surrender of the Confederate ironclad C.S.S. Tennessee. She pounded the Rebel ironclad at point blank range with her four 11-inch guns, cutting Tennessee's steering chains, causing the ironclad to lose all steering control. Perhaps it was the fame brought about by this fight that gave U.S.S. Chickasaw the honor of her own cdv.*

*View 4 shows the U.S.S. Monadnock in her cruise around the Horn of South America, a feat in and of itself for such a low freeboard ship. Of special note in this depiction is the square-rigged mast stepped into the deck ahead of the forward turret. Was this insurance against machinery failure on this long voyage?*

### Talent and frustration

*In addition to the everyday challenges facing an engineer, Chief Engineer Edward D. Robie was assigned two additional and daunting tasks during the war. His well known abilities were needed to solve several design flaws related to the monitors.*

*One problem was with the anti-torpedo raft. This unwieldly contraption was affixed to the bow, offering some protection from underwater mines. The torpedo raft was an utter failure because of its unimaginative design, for which there was no engineering fix.*

*The other task was to assist in the completion of the ultimate monitor, U.S.S. Dictator. Robie's assistance with Dictator did not alter the failure of this machine. The ship was of such an immense size, that the engineering needed to sustain the design was still in the future.*

### Just a little truth

*Commander Donald M. Fairfax was awarded command of the U.S.S. Montauk after John Worden's health failed. Fairfax took Montauk into the April 1863 assault on Ft. Sumter. Slugging it out with the Confederate gunners, the monitors were severely handled by the Rebels leading Fairfax to state:*

I am convinced that although this class of vessel can stand heavy fire, yet the want of more guns will render them harmless before the formidable earthworks and forts. I must say that I am disappointed beyond measure at this experiment of monitors overcoming strong forts. It was a fair trial.

### Call to arms

*John M. Forsyth heard the call to arms early in 1861 beginning a 38 year naval career. He served in the North and South Atlantic Squadrons, the West Gulf Squadron and on the Mississippi River. Some of his time was spent aboard the Passaic class monitor U.S.S.* Catskill, *stationed off Charleston, South Carolina.*

### Confusion reigns

*After John Worden was wounded aboard U.S.S. Monitor, Flag Officer Goldsborough ordered Lt. William N. Jeffers to command Monitor. Unknown at the time of his order, Assistant Secretary of the Navy G.V. Fox had already ordered Lt. Thomas O. Selfridge to command Monitor. However, after four days of command, Selfridge was relieved since it was the flag officer's perogative to name Worden's replacement, not the assistant secretary's.*

*Lt. Jeffer's successful command lasted until August 1862 when he was relieved for ill health. His health was poor enough to keep him from any active combat command for the remainder of the war. With him went the tag of a "brute of a Captain."*

### Bureaucrat & genius supreme

*Engineer Benjamin F. Isherwood was at the top of his profession at the outbreak of the Civil War. It was a war that would radically change the Navy and Isherwood was in the right place at the right time. Included in the design and construction of the monitors from the beginning, he was appointed chief engineer of the Bureau of Steam Engineering early on. In that position he was in an undeniable position of power and authority and was not afraid to promote his own ideas or to butt heads with the likes of Ericsson and high ranking naval officers. He was slandered as an "empire builder" but, if it was so, he was never knocked from his throne. Isherwood was deeply involved in the fiasco of the Casco class monitors, but was successful in washing his hands of the mess and passing the buck, maybe rightfully so, to Alban Stimers.*

*Benjamin F. Isherwood came out of the war with his reputation intact and, along with other engineers such as Ericsson, was "...credited with founding the process of technological research and development in the military."*

## U.S.S. Tecumseh *and* U.S.S. Mannahata (Manhattan)

*Constructed side by side, these two improved Canonicus class monitors would participate together in the Battle of Mobile Bay, August 5, 1864. Tecumseh was launched September 12, 1863, and was shortly followed by the Manhattan on October 14 of the same year.*

*This class of monitor incorporated improvements brought about by the experiences of the Passaic class monitors in battle with the Confederacy. Construction costs soared with last minute changes. Contract disputes over these costs would ride through the courts beyond the end of the war.*

*At Mobile Bay, Tecumseh would meet her violent end from an underwater mine. Manhattan would fight the good fight with the rebel ironclad Tennessee that day. She would survive the war and was not sold out of the naval service until March 1902. Of note in this image is the name board which shows the name, Mannahata, a name that was obviously not to live in association with this monitor.*

### Launching of U.S.S. Camanche

*The U.S.S.* Camanche *was launched in November 1864 in San Francisco Bay, California. She had been originally built as a knocked-down (parts) monitor, and shipped on the merchant ship* Aquilla *to California. The* Aquilla *sank at her pier after arriving in San Francisco, with the monitor still aboard. The monitor's parts were salvaged and reassembled as the vessel in this image. Here she is without her turret and guns. The monitors were launched without their turret or guns, which added an incredible amount of extra weight, and thus were installed only after a successful launch. The Camanche's launching was well attended by the people of San Francisco. Camanche would not be commissioned into naval service until May of the following year, after the war.*

### Camanche's commander

*The portly Charles J. McDougal was the first commander of the first monitor on the west coast of the United States. His command of this unique ironclad was but one of many commands in his long U.S. Navy career. That service would end tragically with his drowning while serving as the light house inspector on the West Coast many years after his uneventful monitor command.*

*Samuel F. Gregory*          *Henry Bulkey*

### A dinosaur and a young pup

*Rear Admiral Samuel F. Gregory's naval career began in the first decade of the 19th century. He was on the retired list as of 1862, but served as the titular head of the office of Superintendent of Iron-Clad Steamers. The department was staffed by engineers who were to give technical direction to the design of steam vessels, steam engines and their components. One of the new breed of naval officers in the office was Second Assistant Engineer Henry Bulkey.*

*These two individuals represented a large number of men, old and young, who provided experience and support for the developing navy, where wind, sail and wood was quickly giving way to iron and steam in such radical machines as the monitors.*

### Commanding a failure

*Someone had to do it, and thus the duty of commanding the failed monitor, U.S.S. Casco, fell onto the shoulders of Acting Master Charles A. Crooker. His monitor without a turret was almost completely useless as a ship of war. It served briefly on the James River and in the Potomac Squadron. Master Crooker's career began with the war in 1861, and ended in 1866. It was a career highlighted by command of a failure.*

**U.S.S. Catskill**

*This image captured a relaxing moment aboard the U.S.S. Catskill. However, her 11-inch and 15-inch guns stand at the ready as well as her two 12-lb brass Dahlgren boat guns. Notice how the 11-inch gun cleared the gun port while the muzzle of the 15-inch gun is clearly within the turret. There was enough room for the 15-inch ball to clear the gun port, but not the gun's muzzle.*

**Commander John Rodgers**

*This image of Commander John Rodgers (seated at center) was taken in San Francisco, California. As the captain of the U.S.S. Monadnock, Rodgers had taken the double turret ironclad along with the U.S.S. Vanderbilt and U.S.S. Powhatan around the horn of South America and up to San Francisco, California in 1866. In April 1866, along the way, Commander Rodgers and his small squadron steamed into Valparaiso, Chile to witness the Spanish fleet shell the city. It was reported that Rodgers had wanted to disrupt and end the bombardment by attacking the Spanish fleet. In particular, Rodgers was thought anxious to attack the Spanish broadside ironclad Numancia to test his four 15-inch guns in turrets against the Spanish ship. To this end he endeavored to enlist the support of the British ships also in the harbor to observe the Spanish attack, but was rebuffed. War with Spain would have to wait a few more years.*

***Monitor crew members. A tale of two classes.***

*Rare among images of the Civil War, is an enlisted man who can be identified to a monitor class ironclad. As a group, enlisted men were less likely to have their photographic likeness recorded.*

*This enlisted man is not identified by name, but his image will always be linked to the monitor U.S.S. Miantonomoh, for the ship's name is visible on his hat.*

*As for the officers, these two views are typical. Seated is Lt. Commander James M. Prichett, commanding the monitor U.S.S. Mahopac. It was an assignment that appears to suit the confidence depicted in his image.*

*With his sword proudly displayed, Master C.M. Schoonmaker would serve as executive officer on U.S.S. Manhattan, taking part in the destruction of the Confederate naval forces.*

**At War's End**

*Two monitors are plainly visible in this image, one of several taken at the end of the war at the Washington Navy Yard. To the left is the Passaic class monitor, U.S.S. Saugus and to the right is the Casco class monitor, U.S.S. Casco. She is a monitor without her turret, clearly demonstrating the utter failure of her entire class, unable to float her turret and guns as designed.*

**Cover-up revealed**

*Daniel Ammen, seen here as a commodore, was well versed in the monitor class vessel. He brought the U.S.S. Patapsco into commission and was her captain until his health failed and he had to relinquish command. Later he would use his experience to bring the double-turret monitor U.S.S. Miantonomoh into commission.*

*In 1883, his book,* The Atlantic Coast, *revealed a Navy Department cover-up from the late war. In part he wrote:*

> In May, 1863, in answer to the requirement of the Navy Department, all of the officers commanding monitors near Charleston (five in number) submitted their opinion in relation to the qualities of that class, which the Department did not think worth while to give to the public in its "Report on Armored Vessels," 1864, made under a Congressional resolution. It might be supposed that this letter had been inadvertently passed over, had it not been on page 603 Captain Ericsson comments upon one of its paragraphs. Captains Drayton and Worden subsequently saw the letter, and concurred in its contents. It has never been published....

*Secretary of the Navy, Gideon Wells, was an advocate of the monitor system. It may have been that the critical letter was just too damning of the monitors for the secretary to release and maintain his position on that class of warship. Reputations and large amounts of money went hand in hand with the monitor class vessels.*

### Surplus supplies of war

*These two stereo images depict no less than seven monitors in two different navy yards at the end of the war. With the war's end there was no reason to keep the monitors in service and they were quickly stripped of their officers and crews and tied-up to rust. Some of the monitors would soon meet with the iron scrapper, and several would be sold to other nations, while most of the remaining ships would rust away for decades. The last was scrapped in 1908.*

## Spanish-American War & the U.S.S. Passaic

In this large albumen image, the U.S.S. Passaic has been brought out of rusting retirement to serve as a harbor defense ship at the outbreak of the Spanish American War. She was over 36 years past her launching and, at this point, only short months away from her final fate of being sold as scrap in October 1899. She was painted white to provide some relief from the heat of summer.

### Yet another Passaic class monitor

*The men and the officers of this old warship stand proud for the New Orleans photographer who captured the scene. The ship is yet another Passaic class monitor brought out of retirement to guard a Southern port as a harbor defense ship at the outbreak of the Spanish-American War. This old monitor, even with its 11-inch thick turret armor, would have been but cannon fodder for any modern warship of 1898.*

## Miantonomoh *on tour*

*The American double-turret monitor, U.S.S. Miantonomoh, is shown at two of her ports of call in Europe. The stern view (right) of the huge monitor was taken in France. She has an awning rigged aft to help protect the crew from the effects of sun upon the poorly ventilated iron.*

*The second, unpublished image (opposite page), captures the monitor at Cronstadt (St. Petersburg), Russia, on Sunday, August 31, 1866. It was wash day on the ship. While in the Russian port, the ship and its officers received a grand state reception that was the talk of the navy for decades.*

*Even prior to* Miantonomoh's *visit, the Russians had been impressed by these American ships. The Russian Navy purchased plans for the Passaic class of monitors and eventually constructed their own monitors.*

## La Onondaga

*This is an interesting dual cdv image of the double turret monitor* La Onondaga *after her sale to the French Navy. In this image, she is crewed by French sailors and poised at Newfoundland awaiting her transatlantic crossing. The French Navy retained this ship's American name and it served until she was sold out of the naval service and broken up for scrap about 1905. As the U.S.S. Onondaga, this ironclad's entire Civil War career had been served on the James River.*

### A relic under steam

*During the Jamestown Naval Review of 1907, the old Passaic class monitor, U.S.S. Canonicus, moves under her own power 44 years after her launching. A true relic of the past century, this old monitor would be sold as scrap in February 1908, the last of the Civil War monitors.*

# Epilogue & More

## Medal of Honor

*Brooklyn Aug 28/65*

*Mr. C.H. Smith*
*Dear Sir,*

*I this day send to you the Medal & accompanying papers sent by the Navy Dept.*

*I congratulate you on receiving this new merited & highly honorable mark of esteem from the U.S. Government.*

*I have shown it to a number of officers in the Navy, who almost envy you such a tribute, & would feel proud if they could have earned and received anything similar.*

*Very Truly & Respectfully*
*E.J. Sherman*

*P.S. I send receipt of express Co. given me for the package. Their charge to you will be .85 cents for delivery.*

Charles H. Smith was a coxswain in the United States Navy serving aboard the side wheel paddle steamer, U.S.S. *Rhode Island*. During the events surrounding the rescue of the crew of the foundering U.S.S. *Monitor,* coxswain Smith and seven other men in *Rhode Island's* first cutter were swept out to sea and supposed to be lost.

In command of the cutter that evening was Acting Masters Mate, D. Rodney Browne, who had promised to return to *Monitor* for a third time to effect the rescue of several remaining souls. Two or three men had refused to leave the sinking ship and had clung, immobile and frozen in terror, to the turret of the doomed ship as

she foundered in the devil's sea. Away from the *Rhode Island* the cutter pulled into the howling storm for *Monitor*, about 2 miles distant, her red distress lantern still visible as the cutter crested wave after wave. But, all was in vain, for as the cutter "...approached what [was] supposed to be position [sic] of the vessel, [Browne] saw nothing but an eddy, apparently produced as [Monitor] went down."[1]

The undermanned cutter was blown out to sea and *Rhode Island* was unable to locate the lost cutter in a search that stretched over several days. However, the crew of the cutter was saved by a passing merchantman under charter to the U.S. government. All eight men were rescued and returned to the care of the United States Navy.

When checking the Medal of Honor records for coxswain Charles H. Smith, he is listed as having his award presented posthumously! However, as is evidenced by this letter, the medal was mailed to him just subsequent to the end of the war. The letter informs Smith that the medal and the citations are being forwarded to him from the care of one Mr. E.J. Sherman. Mr. Sherman refers to the medal as a "...highly honorable mark of esteem from the U.S. Government." Also, Sherman notes the envy with which the medal was reviewed by the Navy officers to whom he showed the item of honor. It must be remembered that as established, the Congressional Medal of Honor was reserved for enlisted men whose bravery in the face of the enemy merited the special notice and thanks of Congress. Officers, no matter how brave their conduct, were not considered for the honor at that time. An officer's bravery was expected by virtue of his commission in the service of the United States.

This letter seems to validate the carelessness of record keeping in the military, and the silliness and ironic absurdity that finds home in the military even to this day. Here, in this informal letter, is the transmittal of the nation's highest award, an honor bestowed by the grateful Congress of the United States. Mailed to the recipient, they expected him to pay the .85 cents postage!

# Letter From the Monitor Boys

*Hampton Roads*
*April 24th 1862*
*U.S. Monitor*

*To our Dear and Honered Captain*
*Dear Sir:*

*These few lines is from your own Crew of the Monitor with there Kindest Love to you there Honered Captain Hoping to God that they will have the pleasure of Welcoming you Back to us again Soon for we are all Ready able and willing to meet Death or any thing else only gives us Back to our Captain again Dear Captain we have got your Pilot house fixed and all Ready for you when you get well again and we all Sincerely hope that soon we will have the pleasure of welcoming you Back to it again for since you left us we have had no pleasure on Board of the Monitor we once was happy on Board of our little Monitor But since we lost you we have Lost our all that was Dear to us still we are waiting very Patiently to engage our Antagonist if we could only get a chance to do so the last time she came out we all thought we would have the Pleasure of Sinking her But we all got Disappointed for we did not fire one Shot and the Norfolk papers Says we are Coward in the Monitor and all we want is a chance to Shew them where it lies with you for our Captain we can teach them who is cowards But there is a great Deal that we would like to write to you But we think you will soon be with us again But we all join in with our Kindest Love to you hoping that God will Restore you to us again and hoping that your Sufferings is at an end now and we are all so glad to hear that your eye Sight will be Spaired to you again, we would wish to write more to you if we have your Permission to do so But at Present we all conclude By tendering to you our Kindest Love and affection to our Dear and Honered Captain.*

*We remain until Death your Affectionate Crew,*
*THE MONITOR BOYS.*[2]

# The Dead Are So Honored

*Tonight we stand face to face with the heros of Hampton Roads. We have met to honor the living; to bless the memory of the dead. These men did not fight for glory, they fought because it was their duty to fight, but glory they shall have. We applaud the living, we drop a tear for those who went down fighting for our flag, but above all, we adopt their widows and orphans as our own.*

Although the above quote was directed to and about the survivors of the destroyed U.S.S. *Congress* and U.S.S. *Cumberland*, it can be applied almost universally to all the brave men who fought either against an ironclad, or in one of the monsters of iron.

*Asst. Surgeon Thomas Danker, drowned aboard U.S.S.* Tecumseh, *August 5, 1864.*

# The Monitor March

Even before the smoke had cleared away from the heavy cannonading, the myth of *Monitor* was born. With disaster averted and a shaky victory in hand, telegraph wires hummed to the frantic and excited clacking of the clerks reporting on the memorial events of March 9, 1862.

The *Virginia* slowly steamed away from her antagonist, *Monitor*. Damaged, but still full of fight, the new captain and the tired crew of *Monitor* stood alone contesting the reappearance of the Rebel ironclad. It was a David and Goliath contest, and although the final blow had not been delivered to the Goliath, *Virginia*, the battlefield was there for the morrow.

Perhaps the most popular means to communicate a myth is through song. Mankind has sung the praises of the glorious, righteous, and noble for thousands of years, including the exploits of the ironclad savior of the Union.

During the Civil War, sheet music was a broad and extensively popular means of mass communication. It allowed the sentiments of the national experience to be fully expressed. Not only did this music present the rousing cadence needed for the dances of the day, but it gave breath to tales of the nation's heroes. Stories were shared by the New England Yankee with his brethren in the plains of Iowa, and all men of our nation at war.

> *Immediately after the famous engagement between the* Monitor *and the* Merrimac, *there was published the "Monitor March," which had a very fine view of the engagement on the back, said to be worth the price of the piece of music, and was sold extensively in Pittsburgh.*[3]

There were more songs about the war, too numerous to count. But, here was the beginning of a myth, a mystique that continues with us, in our national consciousness, to this day.

# Unknown Doorway

What appears to be an elegant doorway at first glance, and out of character with a book on Monitors, becomes a perplexing portal upon close inspection. This is an entrance to a building whose very design visually communicates the building's importance, and most probably the occupants' importance.

Massive, elegant, it forms a pleasing but imposing plan from the palladian window above the balustrade balcony, to doors that appear to be nine or ten feet high. Quoined corners frame a pyramid of steps that reach about six feet above street level. Whoever captured this building on a photographic negative knew exactly

*The mysterious Monitor doorway.*

what he was doing in preserving an image of this masterpiece of stonework, today a monitor mystery.

Under the balcony and flanking the substantial doors are individual plaques which appear to address the image of the ship on the shield above. On closer inspection, the image is of U.S.S. *Monitor*. Just above the ship's image is either 11-inch cannon balls or lighter weight representations of the same size shot which were hurled from the smoothbore Dahlgren guns aboard *Monitor*.

The image of *Monitor* is similar to other *Monitor* portraits that appear on store tokens, Union photographic cases, and other contemporary and somewhat fanciful product interpretations of the ship. Even though there is a considerable amount of written information on the individual plaques, it is unreadable in this photograph.

The nearly mint condition carte de visite has neither a backmark nor any contemporary handwritten identification. Due to its condition, it seems entirely plausible that the little picture resided in an album for years. If a picture is truly worth a thousand words, then this one is worth at least that many questions. Many fanciful and academic considerations can be entertained by staring at the image for a short period of time, and perhaps, that is the beauty of it.

# The Tragedy of '76

Just eleven years after the national fratricide ended, a precariously reunited America celebrated the country's 100th birthday with, among other things, a grand Centennial Exhibition in Philadelphia. Among the wondrous displays of civilization and progress was a mockup monitor turret. Grand and glorious American details were there on display, from the magnificent to the modest. Why was an obsolete naval theme being celebrated? Was it a display of the proud past or a presentation of current might?

The replica turret on public display was an Ericsson turret, which by 1876 was well past any usefulness in war. Even the large cannons were cast iron muzzleloaders left over

from the war, third rate or less when compared with the more modern and lethal breechloading guns of European design and manufacture. During this period, the Civil War hero, David Dixon Porter, Admiral of the Navy, wrote of his beloved service:

*Ericsson may be said to have at one blow destroyed all the squadrons of Europe, for after the engagement between the Monitor and the Merrimac it was plainly to be seen that the old-fashioned wooden vessels were useless for war purposes, although we have held on to our rattle-traps until we are a byword among the nations, a laughingstock even to the Chinese.*[4]

"...even to the Chinese." The Navy had started its dive to the bottom at the end of the Civil War although American technology, through its ironclad navy, looked unassailable. The ships of the greatest fleet on the sea in 1866 were sold at bargain prices as Congress failed to see the need for a substantial navy. Legislators did not fully recognize or appreciate the fact that America had become a world naval power by default and had clearly demonstrated that power to the world.

The Congressional mood had more to do with unfinished business than keeping and building a strong navy. The middle of the American continent had to be tamed, taken away from the Indian, and carved up into proper states and territories. There was also the problem of national reconstruction and retribution; Congress was more intent on dealing with Southern rebels instead of worrying about the French or British and their continued imperial land grab throughout the world.

Neither of the major European countries would consider attacking the U.S. mainland. France demonstrated her commitment to remain in the New World when she pulled the rug from under Maximilian's puppet government in Mexico.

The five years after the war saw much more effort toward creating and passing three Constitutional Amendments by the U.S. Congress than worrying about a fleet. But it would be costly. Congress was the power supreme in America and wanted to keep it that way, even to the extent of their attempt to impeach President An-

*Stereo view of a Monitor turret at the Philadelphia Centennial Exhibition in 1876.*

drew Johnson. This failed by one vote, but it put the executive branch of the government out in the cold until Grant's election.

In 1873 the Spanish Navy stopped the Cuba-bound, American registered ship *Virginius*, and removed her captain, an ex-Confederate naval officer, and 45 men of the 170 persons aboard. Spanish authorities accused the men of assisting the Cuban rebel movement. The men were tried, and of course found guilty. A Spanish firing squad delivered swift punishment.

Congress, the president, and the American people, were incensed. But the reaction was all hot air. Only a small battle-ready navy was available to meet the Spanish on the high seas, to protect troop transports, or to prevent the Spanish fleet from entering U.S. harbors. To commit to battle might be folly. There were no ironclads available to go to sea.

The *Virginius* affair goaded Congress into appropriating funds to finish or update the old monitors. Congress authorized the Secretary of the Navy to use about $900,000 for "reconstruction" of the armored fleet, not nearly enough for ships that had rotted, incomplete, after the end of the Civil War. Five monitors were selected: the still incomplete *Puritan* and the four Miantonomoahs. The old monitors were dismantled and new monitors begun, but they retained the old names since Congress had only authorized reconstruction. Work on the vessels was suspended in 1876. Again, Congress failed to see the need, and renewal of the work would not be authorized again until 1883.

Revised monitor designs of the 1870s and 1880s, although incorporating iron construction and breechloading cannon (both armor and guns forged in British furnaces), were in spirit no more than extrapolated replicas of Civil War ships. Nothing had been learned; but then, nothing needed to be learned. The fate of the monitor concept from 1865 to 1895, when the first oceangoing battleship *Indiana* hoisted colors was decreed by its successful embodiment of inward-looking national values. The *Monitor* was a naval guarantor, as well as the physical protector, of parochial America.

As late as 1888 the U.S. Navy still consisted of little more than wooden cruising ships and gunboats carrying full sail-rigs with auxiliary steam power. Its role was merely to "show the flag" and protect American commercial interests in undeveloped parts of the world. With the Merchant Marine in a state of continual decline except for coastal trade, there was little high seas commerce to protect. The mission to defend the coastal United States was entrusted to Army forts and the isolation provided by wide ocean expanses. The Navy had only a few leftover Civil War monitors rusting "in ordinary."

Although the U.S. Navy was a joke among world navies in the 70s, 80s and early 90s, it was by national choice, a priority of direction never in question, only delayed by the Civil War. The U.S. fleet all but vanished; but men like Mahan, Luce, and Sampson were biding their time in study and development of a new steel navy to come. Arising from the naval ashes of the early 1890s the new fleet would be developed enough to seek revenge on the Spanish Navy in 1898, which had grown decrepit.

Why was America proud of the obsolete turret replica in 1876? The Centennial was a time for national celebration, backslapping and self-congratulatory speeches. America was focused on forging a completed nation from sea to protective sea. Even the loss of Col. George A. Custer and his command added dedication to that effort and reemphasized just how unfinished America really was. It would be another 22 years before the U.S. Navy emerged in a show of force and took her first infant steps as a world power. Though the monitor turret was a great sideshow attraction, the Centennial Celebration of 1876 was in reality not a presentation of America as she wanted to be known to the world, but as she wanted to know herself. The impressive but antiquated gun turret was a promise of sorts. We were strong when we needed to be, and we would be strong again when necessary.

# The Monitor Cyclorama

What is fifty feet high, four hundred feet long, and covered with nearly seven tons of paint? In the late 19th century the appropriate answer would be a Civil War panorama.

French artist Theo. Poilpot was one of several popular painters of the day engaged in battle recreation paintings. These massive sheets of canvas were popular in America and throughout Europe. In the United States today, two of these giant canvases still exist—one in the city of Atlanta and the other in Gettysburg, Pennsylvania, both painted by other well known artists of the day. During the last years of the 1880s through the turn of the century, the height of the panorama craze in the United

States, at least six Civil War battles were represented on canvas and displayed in huge, round buildings specially constructed for the presentation. The Gettysburg panorama was painted four separate times for presentation in four different cities.

One panorama, largely forgotten, is *The Merrimac and Monitor Naval Battle,* painted by Thoe. Poilpot and at least a dozen more craftsman painters. The brochure depicted here is a five cent, fourth edition pamphlet telling the story of the engagement. This fourth edition copy was produced for the showing of that panorama in New York city. It was displayed in a substantial building, four stories high at the internal viewing level, and rising several stories above that to accommodate the hanging of more than twenty thousand square feet of painted surface. This continuous sheet of canvas measured four hundred feet in length by fifty feet in height. Designed to be viewed at the level of the painting's horizon, at about 26 feet above the floor of the painting, its effect was to be three dimensional. The foreground around the base of the painting was,

> ...covered with natural ground, water, grass, trees, and other accessories, so perfectly, that the observer who stands in the centre of it all, cannot discern where the real joins the representation....

The foreground work was important enough to the overall effect to earn credit in the pamphlet. Credit for the New York viewing is given to C.H. Ritter of Chicago. It is difficult to believe that something so large could be but a faded memory today, saved only in a booklet and photographs.

It is not known if this particular painting traveled to various cities, or if there were several executions of the same subject as with the Gettysburg painting. Economy and shared resources suggest, however, that the canvas traveled to several cities, exchanging presentations with other cycloramas. It was just a matter of rolling up the canvas, shipping, and rehanging it at the next stop.

The paintings were afforded no special handling or care. They were vehicles for the collection of admission fees from the general public. *The Merrimac and Monitor Naval Battle* pan-

# BALTIMORE'S GREATEST ATTRACTION !

NOW ON EXHIBITION AT THE

## ✤ CYCLORAMA ✤

Mt. Royal & Maryland Aves., near Union Station.

A VIVID REPRODUCTION OF THE

CELEBRATED NAVAL ENGAGEMENT

—BETWEEN—

# THE MERRIMAC AND MONITOR

SECTIONAL VIEW.

The above is a Sectional View of the Panorama, in which will be found a vivid and realistic representation of the terrific onslaught by the Confederate iron-clad *Merrimac* upon the war ships *Cumberland* and *Congress* of the United States Navy; and also the duel of the *Monitor* and *Merrimac*—the first fight between *iron-clads* in the history of the world.

OPENS 9 A. M.          ADMISSION, 25 CENTS.
CLOSES 10 P. M.        CHILDREN, 15 CENTS.

*A page from a pamphlet for the cyclorama while in Baltimore. It was the next best thing to being there, and only 25 cents.*

346. Monitor and Merrimac Building,
Elitch's Gardens, Denver, Colo.

BATTLE of THE
MONITOR AND MERRIMAC

*Selling the glory of the Civil War in Denver, Colorado.*

*Two sections of the great cyclorama painting depicting* Monitor *and* Virginia *engaged.*

orama was shown in New York at the corner of Madison Avenue and Fifty-Ninth Street, and in St. Paul, Minnesota at the corner of St. Peter and Sixth Streets. Since Poilpot was also involved in panoramas in the cities of Chicago, Illinois and Washington, D.C., it is conceivable that several views rotated among the cities, allowing the greatest exposure possible.

This panorama no longer survives intact. Little is known of its fate, although it is safe to assume that it was cut up and either recycled for its canvas or thrown away. There were stereoscopic photographs recorded of the canvas as it hung in St. Paul, made and published by H.H. Bennett of Kilbourn City, Wisconsin. They were included in a series entitled "Wanderings Among The Wonders and Beauties of Western Scenery." The views were presented on 7x4 inch, yellow stock cards and pictured the panoramic painting in eight cards, numbered 1740-1747. As of August 1990, a small 20 square foot piece of the canvas was reported to exist in private hands in the Winston-Salem, North Carolina area. The aging slice of this once awe-inspiring work depicts Union General Mansfield and his staff, part of the scene represented in the Bennett stereocard #1744.

By 1886, when the pamphlet was published, the U.S. Navy was struggling to emerge from the dark age following the Civil War. Its unprecedented successes in the war, the revolution in American ship design, tactics and strategy, and naval and combined operations warfare, all had been reduced to a popular consumption of "Merrimac and Monitor." The public was interested only in the glories of the fabled past, in the David and Goliath struggle presented on the canvas before them. For the fifty cents admission for adults, twenty-five cents for children, Americans could be entertained by a spectacular, colossal vision of glory.

Undoubtedly, *The Merrimac and Monitor Naval Battle* was a great hit. As the pamphlet describes, a viewer could not "...fail to imagine himself on the very spot, with the actual conflict going on about him."

# ENDNOTES

Opening Quote: Alvah Folsom Hunter, *A Year On A Monitor and The Destruction of Fort Sumter*, Craig L. Symonds, ed. (Columbia, SC: University of South Carolina Press, 1987), 69.

## Building the Machine

1. Robert Erwin Johnson, *Rear Admiral John Rodgers 1812-1882* (Annapolis, MD: United States Naval Institute, 1967), 276.
2. *The Diary of Gideon Wells, Secretary of the Navy Under Lincoln and Johnson* (Boston and New York: Houghton Mifflin Co., 1911), Vol.1, 213.
3. "Letter to the Secretary of the Navy" July 24, 1868, citing the September 16, 1861, *Report of the Board To Examine Plans of Iron-Clad Vessels, Under Act of August 3, 1861.* Hereafter cited as "Letter to the Secretary."
4. Fletcher Pratt, *The Monitor and The Merrimac* (New York: Random House, 1951), 65.
5. "Letter to the Secretary"
6. Edward M. Miller, Lt., USN, *U.S.S. Monitor: The Ship That Launched A Modern Navy* (Annapolis, MD: Leeward Publications, Inc., 1978), 23.
7. Virginius Newton, *The Confederate States Ram Merrimac or Virginia* (Richmond, VA: The Hermitage Press, 1907), 24.
8. *Ibid.*, 27.
9. David D. Porter, *Incidents and Anecdotes of the Civil War* (New York: D. Appleton and Company, 1885), 59.
10. *Ibid.*, 62.
11. *Ibid.*, 62.
12. United States Naval Institute, *Proceedings Magazine*, July 1937, 1021-1022.
13. Spencer Tucker, *Arming the Fleet: U.S. Naval Ordnance in the Muzzle Loading Era* (Annapolis, MD: Naval Institute Press, 1989), 218.
14. *The National Cyclopedia of American Biography* (New York: James T. White & Company, 1898), Vol. II, 112.
15. *Harpers New Monthly Magazine,* No. 148, Vol. 25, 443.
16. *Monitor Collection Catalogue*, Monitor National Marine Sanctuary, National Oceanic and Atmospheric Administration, U.S. Department of Commerce. Papers of Dr. Samuel W. Abbott, No. 01.018.04.1, U.S.S. *Chickasaw.*

## A Few Good Men

1. William C. Davis, *Duel Between the First Ironclads* (Garden City, NY, Doubleday & Company, 1975), 46.
2. R. Gerald McMurty, "The Life and Career of John L. Worden," *Lincoln Herald*, Vol. 51, No.3, Oct. 1949. (Harrogate, TN: Lincoln Memorial University).
3. Joseph Smith Harris Papers, Parry Family Collection, United States Military History Institute, Carlisle Barracks, Pa.
4. Virginius Newton, *The Confederate States Ram Merrimac or Virginia.* (Richmond, VA: The Hermitage Press, 1907), 21.
5. Davis, 129.
6. *Ibid.*, 160.
7. *Ibid.*
8. Edward M. Miller, *U.S.S. Monitor: The Ship That Launched a Modern Navy.* (Annapolis, MD: Leeward Publications, 1978), 69.
9. Robert Thompson & Richard Wainwright, eds. *Confidential Correspondence of Gustavus Gas Fox, Assistant Secretary of the Navy, 1861-1865* (New York: Naval History Society, 1918), Vol. 1, 194-195.
10. James M. Merrill, *DuPont. The Making of an Admiral* (New York: Dodd, Mead & Company 1986), 288.

11. *Ibid.*, 287-288.
12. *Ibid.*, 287-288.
13. *Ibid.*, 286.
14. Gerard Patterson, "Gustave," *Civil War Times Illustrated*, Aug. 1992, 35.
15. James C. Bradford, ed., *Captains of the Old Steam Navy. Makers of the American Naval Tradition 1840-1880* (Annapolis, MD: United States Naval Institute, 1986), 153.
16. *Diary of Gideon Wells, Secretary of the Navy Under Lincoln and Johnson* (Boston and New York: Houghton Mifflin Company, 1911), Vol. 1, 307.
17. Bradford, 158.
18. Robert Erwin Johnson, *Rear Admiral John Rodgers 1812-1882* (Annapolis, MD: United States Naval Institute, 1967), 259.
19. Charles Cowley, *Leaves From A Lawyer's Life Afloat and Ashore*, (Boston, MA: Lee & Shepard, 1879), 123.
20. *Official Records of the Union and Confederate Navies in the War of the Rebellion.* Series I, Vol. 14. (Washington, D.C.: Government Printing Office, 1900), 454. Hereafter cited as *OR, Navy*.
21. Alva F. Hunter, *A Year on a Monitor and the Destruction of Fort Sumter* (Columbia, SC: University of South Carolina Press, 1987), 153.
22. *OR, Navy*, series I, vol. 14, 479.
23. Daniel Ammen, *The Navy In The Civil War—II, The Atlantic Coast* (New York: Charles Scribner's Sons, 1883), 112.
24. *OR, Navy*, series I, vol. 14, 252.
25. E. Milby Burton, *The Seige of Charleston 1861-1865* (Columbia, SC: University of South Carolina Press, 1990), 138.
26. Hunter, 119.
27. *OR, Navy*, series I, vol. 14, 453.
28. *Ibid.*, series I, vol. 14, 290-291.
29. "United States Naval Institute Proceedings," March 1886. *The Monitor Weehawken In the Rebellion*, 117.
30. *OR, Navy*, series I, vol. 14, 291.
31. Pamphlet: *History of the Rebel Ram "Atlanta," Now on Display at Foot of Washington Street*. 23 November 1863. (Philadelphia, PA: Union Volunteer Refreshment Saloon), 8.
32. Johnson, 256.
33. *History of the Rebel Ram "Atlanta," Now on Display at Foot of Washington Street*, 8.
34. *OR, Navy*, series I, vol. 14, 284.
35. Reminiscences of George C. Remey, Rear Admiral, USN, George C. Remey Papers. United States Military History Institute, Carlisle Barracks, Pa.
36. William R. Trotter, *Ironclads and Columbiads. The Civil War in North Carolina. The Coast* (Winston-Salem, NC: John F. Blair, Publisher, 1989), 465.
37. Ammen, 242.
38. *OR, Navy*, series I, vol. 11, 465.
39. William R. Trotter, 313.
40. *OR, Navy*, series I, vol. 16, 173.
41. Ammen, 151.
42. *OR, Navy*, series I, vol. 16, 173.
43. *Ibid.*
44. *Ibid.*
45. *OR, Navy*, series I, vol. 16, 176.
46. *Ibid.*
47. Certificate of Death, 30 June 1889, Navy Department, Bureau of Medicine & Surgery.
48. With special thanks to John Lucky of Richardson, Texas, for research and photographs supplied.

## War Stories

1. E. Milby Burton, *The Seige of Charleston, 1861-1865* (Columbia, S.C.: University of South Carolina Press, 1990), 67.
2. *Ibid.*, 66.
3. *OR, Navy*, Series I, Vol. 21, 578.
4. Letter of P(ierre) Giraud, Lt., U.S.N., U.S.S. *Montauk*, Port Royal, S.C. of July 3, 1863. Private collection.
5. *OR, Navy*. Series I, Vol. 14, 414.
6. *The Civil War Sketchbook of Charles Ellery Stedman, Surgeon, United States Navy* (San Rafael, CA: Presido Press. 1976), 172.
7. *Ibid.*, 134.
8. William R. Trotter, 313.
9. *Letter of Acting Asst. Paymaster Frederick R. Stow, U.S.S. Weehawken, Charleston, S.C., 20 August 1863.* From the Harrisburg Civil War Round Table Collection, United States Military History Institute, Carlisle, Pa.
10. Letter of Acting Asst. Paymaster Frederick R. Stow.
11. *General Order No. 35*, Navy Department, 5 May 1864.
12. *Dorland's Illustrated Medical Dictionary.*
13. General Order No. 35
14. General Order No. 35
15. *OR, Navy*, Series I, Vol. 11, 466.
16. Letter of Acting Asst. Paymaster Frederick R. Stow.
17. Letter of Acting Asst. Paymaster Frederick R. Stow.
18. Robert W. Daley, Ed., *Aboard the U.S.S. Monitor: 1862 The Letters of Acting Paymaster William Frederick Keeler, U.S. Navy To His Wife, Anna* (Annapolis, MD: United States Naval Institute. 1964), 64.
19. Letter of Francis M. Hall, Lt. C.S.A., Fort Sumter, S.C., 11 February 1864 to William Miles, Confederate States Congress. Private collection.

20. C.R.P. Rodgers, Rear Admiral, U.S.N. "DuPont's Attack At Charleston," *Battles and Leaders of the Civil War in 4 Volumes* (New York, Castle Books 1956), Vol. 4, 39.
21. *OR, Navy,* Series I, Vol. 14, 189.
22. *Ibid.,* Series I, Vol. 15, 238-239.
23. *Ibid.,* Series I, Vol. 14, 189.
24. *Ibid.,* Series I, Vol. 15, 28.
25. Arnold A. Putnam, "The Light Draft Monitors of the Civil War" *Naval History Magazine,* May/June 1994, 43.
26. *Ibid.,* 44.
27. Edward William Sloan, *Benjamin Franklin Isherwood, Naval Engineer* (Annapolis, MD: United States Naval Institute Press, 1965), 67.
28. *Ibid.,* 68.
29. Testimony of N. McKay, August 1873, U.S. Court of Claims, Number 6326.
30. *Diary of Gideon Wells, Secretary of the Navy under Lincoln and Johnson* (New York: Houghton Mifflin Company, 1911), Vol. II, 350.
31. *Ibid.*
32. "Launching of a Light Draft Monitor," *Pittsburgh Gazette,* 22 December, 1865.
33. Letter of T. Cooke, 3rd Asst. Engineer, U.S.N., U.S.S. *Onondaga,* James River, Va. of July 14, 1864. Private collection.
34. *OR, Navy,* Series I, Vol. 11, 636.
35. *Ibid.,* Series I, Vol. 11, 662.
36. Charles Crowley, *Leaves From A Lawyers Life Afloat and Ashore* (Boston: Penhallow Printing Company, 1879), 117-118.
37. *OR, Navy,* Series I, Vol. 15, 170.
38. *Ibid.,* 167.
39. Kunhardt, Dorthy Meserve and Philip B. Kunhardt Jr., *Twenty Days* (New York: Castle Books, 1965), 179.
40. "The Assassin's End" *Harper's Weekly. A Journal of Civilization.* 13 May 1865, 294.

## Epilogue & More

1. R. Gerald McMurtry, "The Life & Career of John L. Worden." *The Lincoln Herald,* Oct. 1949, Vol. 51, No. 3, 12.
2. "Reception of the Crews of the *Cumberland* and *Congress*" (New York: Committee of Arrangements, 1862) 15-16.
3. *The Waterways Journal,* September 1, 1928.
4. Porter, David D., *Incidents and Anecdotes of the Civil War* (New York: D. Appleton and Company, 1885), 63.

# REFERENCES CITED OR CONSULTED

**Books**

Amadon, George F. *Rise of the Ironclads.* Missoula, MT: Pictorial Histories Publishing Co., 1988.

Ammen, Daniel, Rear Admiral U.S.N. *The Atlantic Coast.* New York: Charles Scribner's Sons, 1883.

*Battles and Leaders of the Civil War.* New York: The Century Company, 1887.

Bennett, Frank M. *The Steam Navy of the United States: A History of the Growth of the Steam Vessels of War in the U.S. Navy, and of the Naval Engineering Corps.* Pittsburg, PA: Warren & Company, 1896.

Berent, Irwin M. *The Crewmen of the U.S.S. Monitor. A Biographical Directory.* North Carolina Department of Cultural Resources, 1983.

Boynton, Charles B. *History of the Navy During the Rebellion.* New York: D. Appleton and Company, 1867.

Bradford, James C., ed. *Admirals of the New Steel Navy. Makers of the American Naval Tradition.* Annapolis, MD: Naval Institute Press, 1990.

_____. *Captains of the Old Steam Navy. Makers of the American Naval Tradition.* 1840-1880, Annapolis, MD: Naval Institute Press, 1986.

Bradshaw, Timothy Eugene, Jr. *Battery Wagner, The Seige, The Men Who Fought, and The Casualties.* Columbia, SC: Palmetto Historical Works, 1993.

Browne, Samuel T. *First Cruise of the Montauk, Personal Narratives of the Events In the War of the Rebellion.* No.1, Second Series, Providence, RI: The N. Bangs Williams Co., 1880.

Browning, Robert M. *From Cape Charles to Cape Fear: The North Atlantic Blockading Squadron during the Civil War.* Tuscaloosa, AL: University of Alabama Press, 1993.

Burton, E. Milby. *The Siege of Charleston.* Columbia, SC: University of South Carolina Press, 1970.

Butts, Frank B. *My First Cruise At Sea and the Loss of the Iron-Clad Monitor: Personal Narratives of the War of the Rebellion.* No. 4.

Callahan, Edward W., ed. *List of Officers of the Navy of the United States and of the Marine Corps from 1775 to 1900.* New York: L. R. Hamersly & Company, 1901.

Canfield, Eugene B. *Civil War Naval Ordnance.* Washington, DC: United States Government Printing Office, 1969.

Canney, Donald L. *The Old Steam Navy, Frigates, Sloops, and Gunboats, 1815-1885.* Annapolis, MD: Naval Institute Press, 1990.

_____. *The Old Steam Navy, The Ironclads, 1842-1885.* Annapolis, MD: Naval Institute Press, 1993.

Church, William Conant. *The Life of John Ericsson.* 2 Vols. New York: Charles Scribner's Sons, 1906.

Coggins, Jack. *Arms and Equipment of the Civil War.* Garden City, NY: Doubleday & Company, Inc., 1962.

Coski, John M. *Capital Navy, The Men, Ships and Operations of the James River Squadron.* Campbell, CA: Savas Woodbury Publishers, 1996.

Daly, Robert W., ed. *Aboard the USS Monitor: 1862. The Letters of Acting Paymaster William Frederick Keeler, U. S. Navy to His Wife, Anna.* Annapolis, MD: United States Naval Institute, 1964.

Davis, William C., ed. *The Image of War 1861-1865.* Garden City, NY: Doubleday & Company, Inc., 1981.

*Diary of Gideon Wells, Secretary of the Navy Under Lincoln and Johnson.* 3 Vols. Boston and New York: Houghton Mifflin Company, 1911.

Dickerson, Edward N. *The Navy of the United States: An Exposure of its Condition, and The Causes of Its Failures.* New York: 1864.

Donovan, Frank. *The Ironclads.* New York: A. S. Barnes and Company, Inc., 1961.

Farragut, Loyall. *The Life of David Glasgow Farragut, First Admiral of the United States Navy, Embodying His Journal and Letters.* New York: D. Appleton and Company,1879.

*Firefight on the Chesapeake Bay.* Richmond, VA: Lyceum Publications, 1976.

Franklin, S. R., Rear-Admiral U.S. Navy, Ret. *Memories of A Rear-Admiral Who Has Served for More than Half a Century in the Navy of the United States.* New York: Harpers and Brothers Publishers, 1898.

*General Orders No. 35.* Navy Department, May 5, 1864, Gideon Wells, Secretary of the Navy.

Gibbons, Tony. *Warships and Naval Battles of the Civil War.* New York: Gallery Books, 1989.

Hammersly, Lewis R. *The Records of Living Officers of the U.S. Navy and Marine Corps.* Philadelphia: J. B. Lippincott & Company, 1870 & 1878.

Hensel, W. U. *Buchanan's Administration on the Eve of the Rebellion.*

*History of the Rebel Steam Ram Atlanta.* Philadelphia, PA: Union Volunteer Refreshment Saloon, 1863.

Hoehling, A. A. *Damn the Torpedoes! Naval Incidents of the Civil War.* Winston-Salem, NC: John F. Blair, 1989.

Hunt, Cornelius E. *The Shenandoah; or the Last Confederate Cruiser.* New York: G. W. Carleton, & Co., 1867.

Hunter, Alvah Folsom. *A Year on a Monitor and the Destruction of Fort Sumter.* Craig L. Symonds, ed. Columbia, SC: University of South Carolina Press, 1987.

Johnson, Robert Erwin. *Rear Admiral John Rodgers, 1812-1882.* Annapolis, MD: United States Naval Institute, 1967.

King, Rear Admiral Randolph W., USN (Ret.), ed. *Naval Engineering and American Seapower.* Baltimore, MD: The Nautical & Aviation Publishing Company of America, Inc., 1989.

Lambert, Andrew. *Warrior: The World's First Ironclad Then and Now.* Annapolis, MD: Naval Institute Press, 1987.

Lewis, Charles Lee. *Admiral Franklin Buchanan: Fearless Man of Action.* Baltimore, MD: The Norman, Remington Company, 1929.

Lewis, Emanuel. *Seacoast Fortifications of the United States: An Introductory History.* Annapolis, MD: Leeward Publications, 1979.

Littleton, William G. *The Cumberland, the Monitor and the Virginia.* Philadelphia: William G. Littleton, 1933.

Loubat, J. F. *Narrative of the Mission to Russia, In 1866, of the Hon. Gustavus Vasa Fox, Assistant-Secretary of the Navy.* New York: D. Appleton & Company, 1879.

MacBride, Robert. *Civil War Ironclads: The Dawn of Naval Armor.* Philadelphia and New York: Chilton Books, 1962.

Mahan, Alfred T. *The Gulf and Inland Waters: The Navy in the Civil War.* Reprint. Freeport, NY: Books for Libraries Press, 1970.

Mahan, A. T., Capt. *The Influence of Sea Power Upon History 1660-1783.* Boston: Little Brown & Company, 1898.

Meade, Rebecca Paulding. *Life of Hiram Paulding, Rear Admiral, U.S.N.* New York: The Baker & Taylor Company, 1910.

Merrill, James M. *DuPont, The Making of an Admiral.* New York: Dodd, Mead & Company, 1986.

_____. *Battle Flags South: The Story of the Civil War Navies on Western Waters.* Cranbury, NJ: Associated University Presses, Inc., 1970.

Miller, Edward M., Lt., USN. *U.S.S. Monitor: The Ship That Launched A Modern Navy.* Annapolis, MD: Leeward Publications, Inc., 1978.

Mills, Eric. *Chesapeake Bay in the Civil War.* Centerville, MD: Tidewater Publishers, 1996.

*Monitors of the U.S. Navy.* Navy Department, Naval History Division. Washington, D.C.: Government Printing Office, 1969.

Newton, Virginius. *The Confederate States Ram Merrimac or Virginia.* Richmond, VA: The Hermitage Press, 1907.

*Officers of the Army and Navy (Regular and Volunteer) Who Served in the Civil War.* Philadelphia, PA: L.R. Hammersly & Co., 1894.

*Official Records of the Union and Confederate Navies in the War of the Rebellion.* 31 Vols. Washington, D.C.: Government Printing Office, 1895–1929.

*Ordnance Instructions for the United States Navy.* Washington, DC: Government Printing Office, 1866.

*Outstanding Events In U.S. Naval History.* U.S. Navy Recruiting Service Publication, NRB-28344-11-13-40-200M, 1940.

Page, Dave. *Ship Versus Shore: Civil War Engagements Along Southern Shores and Rivers.* Nashville, TN: Rutledge Hill Press, 1994.

Porter, David D. *Incidents and Anecdotes of the Civil War.* New York: D. Appleton and Company, 1885.

_____. Admiral, U.S.N. *The Naval History of the Civil War.* New York: The Sherman Publishing Company, 1886.

*Reception of the Crews of the Cumberland and Congress.* New York: Published by the Committee of Arrangements, 1862.

*Register of the Commissioned, Warrant, and Volunteer Officers of the Navy of the United States Including Officers of the Marine Corps and Others, to January 1, 1865.* Washington, D.C.: Government Printing Office, 1865.

*Report on the Secretary of the Navy, with An Appendix Containing Reports From Officers.* December 1864. Washington, D.C.: Government Printing Office, 1864.

Reynolds, Clark G. *Famous American Admirals.* New York: Van Nostrand Reinhold Company, 1978.

*Sale of Iron-Clads.* 40th Congress, 2d Session, Report No. 64.

Selfridge, Thomas O., Jr., *What Finer Tradition: The Memoirs of Thomas O. Selfridge, Jr., Rear Admiral, U.S.N.* William N. Still, Jr., ed. Columbia, SC: University of South Carolina Press, 1987.

Silverstone, Paul H. *Warships of the Civil War Navies.* Annapolis, MD: Naval Institute Press, 1989.

Sloan, Edward William, III. *Benjamin Franklin Isherwood, Naval Engineer: The Years as Engineer In Chief, 1861-1869.* Annapolis, MD: United States Naval Institute, 1965.

Sprout, Harold and Margaret. *The Rise of American Naval Power, 1776-1918.* Annapolis, MD: Naval Institute Press, 1966.

*Statistical History of John Ridgway's Vertical Revolving Battery, With Drawings.* Boston: Prentiss & Deland, 1865.

Steadman, Charles Ellery. *The Civil War Sketchbook of Charles Ellery Steadman, Surgeon, United States Navy.* San Rafael, CA: Presidio Press, 1976.

Still, William N., Jr., *Monitor Builders: A Historical Study of the Principle Firms and Individuals Involved in the Construction of the USS Monitor.* Washington, DC: National Maritime Initiative, Division of History, National Park Service, Department of the Interior, 1988.

_____. *Ironclad Captains: The Commanding Officers of the USS Monitor.* Washington, DC: Marine and Estuarine Management Division, National

Oceanic and Atmospheric Administration, United States Department of Commerce. U.S. Government Printing Office, 1988.

*The Merrimac and Monitor Naval Engagement.* New York: Panorama Company, 1886.

*The National Cyclopedia of American Biography.* 25 Vols., New York: James T. White & Company, 1898.

*The National Cyclopedia of American Biography.* 27 Vols. New York: James T. White & Company, 1921.

*The Monitor. Its Meaning and Future.* Papers from a National Conference, Raleigh, NC: April 2-4, 1978, Washington, D.C.: The Preservation Press, 1978.

Thompson, Robert Means and Richard Wainwright, eds. *Confidential Correspondence of Gustavus Vasa Fox Assistant Secretary of the Navy 1861-1865.* New York: Naval History Society, 1920.

Trotter, William R. *Ironclads and Columbiads: The Civil War in North Carolina, The Coast.* Winston-Salem, NC: John F. Blair, Publisher, 1989.

Tucker, Spencer. *Arming the Fleet: U.S. Navy Ordnance in the Muzzle-Loading Era.* Annapolis, MD: Naval Institute Press, 1989.

White, E.V. *The First Iron-Clad Naval Engagement In The World.* New York: J.S. Ogilvie Publishing Company, 1906.

White, William Chapman and Ruth White. *Tin Can on a Shingle.* New York: E.P. Dutton & Company, Inc., 1958.

Wideman, John C. *Naval Warfare: Courage and Combat on the Water.* New York:

Wilson, H. W. *Ironclads In Action: A Sketch of Naval Warfare from 1855 to 1895.* 2 Vols. London: Sampson Low, Marston and Company, Ltd., 1896.

"Letter From The Secretary of the Navy." *Rebel Ram Albemarle.* 38th Congress, 1st. Session, Ex. Doc. No. 83, House of Representatives.

**Periodicals**

*Paper read before the Cliosophic Society.* Lancaster, PA: Jan. 24, 1908.

"Iron Clad Vessels." *Harper's New Monthly Magazine.* Sept. 1862.

"The First Cruise of the 'Monitor' Passaic." *Harper's New Monthly Magazine.* Oct. 1863.

"The Last Cruise of the Monitor." *The Atlantic Monthly*, Mar. 1863.

"Memorial of Charles W. Whitney, For Relief, In Building The Iron-Clad Battery, "KEOKUK," 25 Per Cent. Larger Than Agreed Upon, When Price Was Named, And For Which No Compensation Has Been Paid." (NP) New York.1868.

*Lincoln Herald.* Oct. 1946, Vol. 48, No. 3.

"John L. Worden—Prisoner of War." R. Gerald McMurtry. *Lincoln Herald.* Oct. 1948, Vol. 50, No. 3.

"The Life and Career of John L. Worden." R. Gerald McMurtry. *Lincoln Herald.* Oct. 1949, Vol. 51, No. 3.

*Harpers New Monthly Magazine.* No. 148. Vol. 25.

"Gustave." Gerald Patterson. *Civil War Times Illustrated.* Aug. 1992, 32.

Frederick Stow, unpublished papers. The Harrisburg Civil War Roundtable Collection; U.S. Military History Institute, Carlisle Barracks, Pa.

**Articles from Naval Institutes *Proceedings Magazine.***

"Sunken Union Ship to be Raised." (NKB) Nov. 1967, 151.

"U.S.S. Tucumseh: Treasure in Mobile Bay." J. Stokesberry. Aug. 1968, 147.

"Blue Water Monitor." James Knowles, Jr. Mar. 1973, 78.

"A Modified Monitor." W. I. Chambers. Oct-Dec. 1881, 437.

"At Sea In A Monitor." F. M. Holbrook. Apr. 1964, 164.

"American Monitors." P. R. Osborn. Feb. 1937, 235.

"An Early Dreadnought: Letter of W. B. Wetmore." Jul-Sept. n.d., 855.

"Onondaga." (NA) May 1931, 633.

"Penetration of Wrought-Iron Plates." Apr.-June 1885, 341.

"Monitor Weehawken in the Rebellion." B. W. Lorning. Apr.-June 1886, 111. "Monitor Patapsco." E. K. Thompson. Dec. 1968, 524.

"The Light Draft Monitors of the Civil War." Arnold A. Putnam. May-June 1994, 42.

Unpublished papers of Dr. Samuel Warren Abbott, U.S.N. No. 01.018.03.2 U.S.S. *Catskill.* "Reminiscences of IronClad Life." Read at Wakefield in 1891, Feby., before Post 12, G.A.R.

"Reminiscences of George C. Remey, Rear Admiral U.S.N." George C. Remey Papers, U. S. Army Military History Institute, Carlisle Barracks, Pa.

"Memoir." Joseph Smith Harris Papers. Parry Family Collection, U. S. Army Military History Institute, Carlisle Barracks, Pa.

**Monitor Collection Catalogue, Monitor National Marine Sanctuary, National Oceanic and Atmospheric Administration, U. S. Department of Commerce:**

G.01.018.03.2 Catskill
G.01.018.04.1 Chickasaw
G.01.018.07.1 Miantonomoh
G.01.018.01.2 Miantonomoh
G.01.018.09.1 Monadnock
G.01.018.16.1 Weehawken
G.01.018.18.1 Scorpion
G.01.018.

# INDEX

Adams, Henry A., command of US naval forces off Ft. Pickens, Fl., 24

Albany Iron Works, ironplate maker for USS *Monitor*, 18

Alps, coal tug, mentioned, 62

Alston, J. Julius, Confederate gun commander in Ft. Wagner, 34

Ammen, Daniel, comments on "Davids", 54; and comments on torpedoes, 56; and photograph, 85

*Atlanta*, C.S.S., mentioned, 58; and poem about capture, 38; and photographed in Philadelphia, 37; and devastation of by 15-inch gunfire from U.S.S. *Weehawken* (monitor), 37; and prejudiced description of crew, 38

Bailey, escaped slave officer's servant aboard U.S.S. *Weehawken* (monitor), 51

Bankhead, John P., last to command U.S.S. *Monitor*, 28; and later career, 29; and photograph, 29

Barbot, Lieutenant, Confederate States Forces, first to open fire on U.S.S. *Weehawken* (monitor), 37

Barnes, Joseph Dr., performs autopsy on John W. Booth on deck of U.S.S. *Montauk* (monitor), 68

Bashford, Andrew P., aboard U.S.S. *Patapsco* (monitor), 41; and death 44; and photograph, 41

Beaufort, South Carolina, a rest and relaxation center for Union Navy, 47

Beauregard, P.T.G., restored to favor by his defense of Charleston, South Carolina, 31

Belknap, George E., votes to renew attack on Charleston , 33; and written recognition of Edward Decker, pilot, 40

Booth, John Wilkes, hard death, 67; and post mortem illustration, 69; and photograph, 68

Boston Navy Yard, photograph, 59

Bragg, Braxton Bragg, Commanding Confederate forces at Pensacola, Fl., 24

Brilliant, steamer, mentioned, 62

Brooklyn Navy Yard, photograph, 21

Browne, D. Rodney, rescue of Monitor's crew, 91

Buchannan, Franklin, goes South, 36; and surrenders the ironclad C.S.S. *Tennessee* (ironclad), 47

Bulkey, Henry, photograph, 82

Bushnell, Charles, naval constructor, 7; and with Lincoln presenting Ericsson's plans, 16

Butler, Benjamin, mentioned, 58; and aboard U.S.S. *Onondaga* (monitor), 63

Camanche, U.S.S. (monitor), photographs, 71; and 81

Carpenter, Charles, takes command of U.S.S. *Catskill* (monitor) during combat, 35; and mentioned 44

*Canonicus*, U.S.S. (monitor), mentioned, 50; and James River war photograph, 73; and 1907 naval review photograph, 89

*Casco*, U.S.S. (monitor), photograph of a failed monitor, 61

*Catskill*, U.S.S. (monitor), high causality rate aboard, 49; and photograph, 83

Centennial Exhibition, Philadelphia, discussed in relation to naval exhibit, 94

*Chickasaw*, U.S.S. (monitor), illustration, 77

*Chimo*, U.S.S. (monitor), failure realized upon launching, 60

Cillery Greenleaf, comments upon Charleston Harbor picket duty, 56

City Point, Virginia, need for protection as base of operations, 64

Cock of the *Weehawken*, short description, 65; and illustration, 66

*Conemaugh*, U.S.S. steamer, mentioned, 41

*Congress*, U.S.S., destroyed in battle with Confederate ironclad C.S.S. *Virginia*, 26, 76; and survivors honored, 92

Corbett, Boston, ignores orders, shoots and mortally wounds John W. Booth, 67

Corning, Erastus, Industrialists helping the war effort, 18; and photograph, 18

cover-up, monitor class weakness and failures withheld from United States Congress, 85

Craven, T. M., In command of U.S.S. *Tecumseh* (monitor) 56; and photograph 57

Crooker, Charles A., commanding U.S.S. *Casco* (monitor), photograph, 82

*Cumberland*, U.S.S., destroyed in battle with Confederate ironclad C.S.S. *Virginia*, 26, 76; and mentioned, 51; and survivors honored, 92

Custer, George A., mentioned, 96

Dahlgren, John, takes command of South Atlantic Blockading Squadron, 32; and laments death of George W. Rodgers, 35; and orders with regards to Confederate "Davids" 54-55; and photograph, 32

Dahlgren Shell Gun, concept and construction of the 15-inch smooth bore naval gun, 20

Dahlgren boat howitzer, photograph, 23

*Dandelion* (tug), removes dead and wounded from U.S.S. *Catskill* (monitor), 35

Danker, Thomas, drowned aboard U.S.S. *Tecumseh* (monitor), photograph, 92

"Davids", Confederate semi submersible torpedo boats, 54; and photograph, 55

Davis, Charles, member of the Ironclad Board, 15; and belittles Ericsson's ironclad plans, 16; and photograph, 16

Decker, Edward A., pilot of U.S.S. *Canonicus* (monitor), 39; and photograph, 40

DeLuce, Theodore wounded in action aboard U.S.S. *Montauk* (monitor) 75

*Devastation*, H.M.S. (British ironclad), refuses to join in proposed attack on Spanish fleet, 65

Dickinson, Charles, artist of naval sketch off Seabrook Island, South Carolina, 74

*Dictator*, U.S.S. (monitor), John Rodgers takes command of Ericsson's troubled monitor, 39

Downing Street, a direct threat by John Ericsson to the English navy, 20

DuPont, Samuel Francis, unapologetic career 29; and photograph, 30

**E**ricsson, John, direct presentation of monitor concept to Commander Davis, 17; and opinion on Commander Porter's inspection of Monitor, 19; and refuses to assist with Casco (Yazoo) monitor class ships, 58; and photograph, 14

Executions, by Spanish officials of US citizens for gun running, 95

**F**airfax, Donald, mentioned as commander of U.S.S. *Montauk* (monitor), 46; and photograph, 78

Farragut, David G., at Mobile Bay, 58

Fenton, Andrew, last documented survivor of U.S.S. *Monitor*, 45

Fenwick, James, washed overboard during the sinking of U.S.S. *Monitor* off Cape Hatteras, 28

Foot, Andrew, unexpected death, 30; and temperance movement in the U.S. Navy, 51; and photograph, 52

Forsyth, John M., mentioned aboard U.S.S. *Catskill* (monitor), 78

Fort Darling, U.S. naval assault on Richmond, Virginia stopped at Drewry's Bluff fortification, 36

Fort Fisher, North Carolina fort mentioned in battle with U.S.S. *Canonicus* (monitor), 40

Fort Wagner, Charleston harbor fort mentioned in battle with U.S.S. *Catskill* (monitor), 34

Fox, Gustavus Vasa, at Ft. Monroe, 17; and impressed with 15-inch gun, 21; and friend of DuPont, 30-31; and opinion about Chief Engineer Alban Stimers, 59

*Franklin*, U.S.S., receiving ship mentioned, 44

*Fredericksburg*, C.S.S. (ironclad), mentioned, 63; and passes James River obstructions, 64,

**G**alena, U.S.S. (ironclad), mentioned, 16; and under command of John Rodgers, 36

Giraud, Pierre, author of revealing letter, 46; and receives the sword of Confederate Admiral Franklin Buchannan in surrender, 47; and complete text of letter, 48

Grant, Ulysses S., aboard U.S.S. *Onondaga* (monitor), 63

Green, Samuel D., takes command of U.S.S. *Monitor* after Worden's wounding, 26

Gregory, Francis H., superintendent of ironclads, 59; and photograph, 82

**H**all, Francis H., Confederate Assistant Engineer mentioned, 52

Harlin, W.H., Surgeon dismissed from service for covering-up abuse, 50

Harper's Magazine, article on the debate of gun power verses armor strength, 22

*Housatonic*, U.S.S., mentioned, 54

Herold, David, mentioned, 67; and held as prisoner aboard U.S.S. *Montauk* (monitor), 69

**I**ronclad Board, mentioned, 15

Isherwood, Benjamin F., photograph, 79

**J**ones, Edward, Acting Master dismissed from the Navy for abuse of an enlisted man, 50

Jeffers, William M., photograph, 79

John S. Ide, steamer assigned to transport John W. Booth to Washington Navy Yard, 68

**K**eeler, William F., mentioned in relation to grog ration aboard U.S.S. *Monitor*, 52

*Kekouk*, U.S.S.(ironclad), in action before Charleston , 30-31; and illustration, 53; and sustains severe and fatal damage, 54

Kennison, William, in action aboard U.S.S. *Cumberland* against C.S.S. *Virginia*, 76, photograph, 76

**L**a*Onondaga* (monitor), photograph of U.S.S. *Onondaga* (monitor) after sale to the French Navy, 89

Lee, Samuel P., commanding North Atlantic Blockading Squadron, 64

light draft monitors, failure, 58

Lincoln, Abraham, presenting the Ericsson ironclad, 16; and remarks with regards to efficiency of DuPont at Charleston, 30; and cracking jokes aboard U.S.S. *Onondaga* (monitor), 63

**M**cCellan, George, Pen$inular campaign hampered by Confederate naval forces, 17

McDougal, Charles J., photograph of commander of U.S.S. *Camanche* (monitor), 81

*Manhatten*, U.S.S.(monitor), photograph under construction, 80

Medal of Honor, transmittal letter for U.S.S. *Monitor* crew member, 91

*Miantonomoh*, U.S.S (monitor), photographed at Charlestown Navy Yard, 71; and in France, 89; and in Cronstadt, Russia, 90

Miles, William P., Confederate States Congressman mentioned, 53

Miller, Joseph N., votes to renew ironclad assault on Charleston forts, 33

*Minnesota*, U.S.S., hard aground in Hampton Roads, 26; and mentioned, 76

*Monadnock*, U.S.S. (monitor), cruise to San Francisco, 39; and John Rodgers takes command, 39; and illustration, 77; and photographed in the San Francisco Navy Yard, 71

*Monitor*, U.S.S., mentioned, 16; and 100 day contract for,17; and naming thereof, 20; and near disaster on first voyage, 25; and her loss at sea, 28-29; and fake photograph, 62; and assault on Fort Darling, Drewery's Bluffs, 77

"Monitor Boys", letter from crew of U.S.S. *Monitor* to John Worden, 92

monitor class, living conditions below deck, 48; and low morale, 49; and discipline aboard, 49

monitor class descriptions: COASTAL MONITORS; *Canonicus*, 9; and *Dictator*, 11; and *Kalamazoo*, 10; and *Miantonomoh*, 10; and *Monitor*, 8; and *Onondaga*, 12; and *Passaic*, 8; and *Puritan*, 11; and *Roanoke*, 11; and *Yazoo*, 9; and RIVER MONITORS: *Marietta*, 13; and *Milwaukee*,13; and *Neosho*, 13; and *Ozark*, 13

Monitor Cyclorama, a description and discussion, 96; and pamphlet 97; and illustration of 2 panels, 98; and post card illustration, 98

"Monitor March", sheet music, 93

monitor turret, mock-up at Philadelphia Centennial Exhibition, 1876, 94

*Montauk*, U.S.S. (monitor), new command for John Worden, 27; and in the Washington Navy Yard photograph, 67; and Lincoln aboard, 67; and under construction photograph, 72

Moultrie House, mentioned, 56

MuMutrie, Daniel, surgeon aboard U.S.S. *Sangamon* (monitor) photograph, 75

*Nahant*, U.S.S. (monitor), pilothouse weakness, 35; and adjudication of prize money dispute, 38; and crew disability, 49

*New Ironsides*, U.S.S. (broadside ironclad), mentioned, 16, 54; and before Charleston, South Carolina, 30-31; and attacked by torpedo boat, 56

Nicholson, James W. A., in command of U.S.S. *Manhatten* (monitor), 22

Northern newspapers: DuPont asks them not to report on monitor damage, 35

*Numancia*, Spanish naval vessel, 39

*Oleander*, U.S.S., mentioned, 41

*Onondaga*, U.S.S.(monitor), on the James River, 63; and photograph, 64; and retires in face of Confederate naval attack, 65

*Parker*, William A., commanding U.S.S. *Onondaga* (monitor), 64; and dismissal from the Navy, 65

*Passaic*, U.S.S. (monitor), mentioned, 63; and under construction photograph, 72; and illustration, 77; and 1898 photograph, 87

Passaic Class Monitor, illustration, 53; and 1898 photograph, 88

*Patapsco*, U.S.S. (monitor), destruction by torpedo, 41-43

"patriotic cover", illustration of battle between U.S.S. *Monitor* and C.S.S. *Virginia*, 45

Paulding, Hiram, member of Ironclad Board, 15

Philadelphia Centennial Exhibition of 1876, mock-up of a monitor turret, photograph, 95

pilothouse, weakness of, 35

Poilpot, Theo., artist of *Monitor* and *Merrimac* panorama painting, 96

Port Royal, South Carolina, seen as coaling station for U.S. Navy, 29, 46

Porter, David D., inspects U.S.S. *Monitor*, 19; and photograph, 19; and order to close with rebel forts at Wilmington, North Carolina, 39; mentioned, 94

*Powhatten*, U.S.S., in concert with U.S.S. *Monadnock* (monitor), 39

Prichett, James M., photograph, 84

prostitution, mentioned at Beaufort, South Carolina, 47

*Puritan*, U.S.S. (monitor), mentioned, 95

*Quackenbush*, S.P., photograph, 43

Quintard, G.W., naval constructor, 64

*Randall*, William P., photograph, 76; and in action aboard U.S.S. *Cumberland*, 76

repair shops, for U.S. naval vessels at Port Royal, 47

*Rhode Island*, U.S.S., towing U.S.S. *Monitor* off Cape Hatteras during storm, 28; and rescuing crew members of the sinking U.S.S. *Monitor*, 91

*Richmond*, C.S.S. (ironclad), mentioned, 63; and runs aground on obstructions in James River, 65

Robie, Edward D., photograph, 78; and mentioned , 78

Rodgers, George, rejoins his prior command for the last time, 33: and killed in action aboard U.S.S. *Catskill* (monitor), 34

Rodgers, John, early life, 35-36; and photograph 36; and proposes to attack Spanish ironclad *Numancia* at Valparaiso, Chile, 39; and in group photograph, 83

Rodman process: used to construct 15-inch naval gun, 21

*Sachem*, U.S.S., near disaster while towing U.S.S. *Monitor* off the Delaware coast, 26

*Sangamon*, U.S.S. (monitor), photographs, 20, 70, 73

Sampson, William T., aboard the U.S.S. *Patapsco* (monitor), 41-42; and photograph, 42

Schoonmaker, C.M., photograph, 84

*Shawnee*, U.S.S. (monitor), mentioned, 58; and photograph, 59

Sherman, Willaim T. bypasses Charleston, South Carolina, 33

Smith, Charles H., receives the Medal of Honor for actions related to rescuing crew members of U.S.S. *Monitor*, 91

Smith, Joseph, offers command of U.S.S. *Monitor* to John Worden, 25; as member of Ironclad Board, 15, 51; and photograph, 16

Stanton, Edwin, as Secretary of War and his orders regarding disposition of John W. Booth's body, 68

Stimers, Alban, as Chief Engineer and his connection with a monitor class failure, 59; and intoxicated by importance, 60; and photograph, 60

Stocking, John, washed overboard during U.S.S. *Monitor's* sinking, 28

Stodder, Louis P., cutting U.S.S. *Monitor* loose from towing ship during the storm, 28; and photograph, 27

Stuyvesant, Moses S., photograph, 76

Surgeons: duty aboard the monitors, 75

surplus monitors, photographs of, 86

*Tallaposa*, U.S.S., mentioned, 44

Taylor, John C., photographer's studios faking photographs of U.S.S. *Monitor*, 62

*Tecumseh*, U.S.S. (monitor), mentioned, 42; and short service, 56-57; and photograph under construction, 80

*Tennessee*, C.S.S. (ironclad), faces the 15-inch guns of U.S. Navy monitor, 22; and mentioned, 56, 77

Thompson, Thomas, abuse by officers aboard an ironclad monitor, 50; and injured by gun recoil, 51

Thurston, Lieutenant, Confederate officer wounded at his gun aboard C.S.S. *Atlanta* (Ironclad), 37

torpedoes (underwater mines), U.S.S. *Patapsco* (monitor) dragging for same, 42

torpedo boat (Davids), mentioned, 55

Truscott, Peter, wounded in action in U.S.S. *Catskill's* pilothouse, 34

turret: Confederate gunners demonstrate knowledge of weakness, 40; and interior view illustration, 50

*Tuscarcra*, U.S.S., in concert with U.S.S. *Monadnock* (monitor), 39

*Umpqua*, U.S.S.(monitor) a near disaster during her launching, 62

Unknown Doorway: with monitor plaques on either side, photograph, 93

*Vanderbilt*, U.S.S., in concert with U.S.S. *Monadock* ( monitor), 39

*Virginia*, C.S.S. (ironclad), conversion from the U.S.S. *Merrimac*, 15; and battle of March 8, 1862, 26

*Virginia II*, C.S.S.(ironclad), mentioned, 63; and runs aground, 64; and struck over 75 times in battle, 65

Virginius Affair, post Civil War Navy not ready for war with Spain, 95

*Wabash*, U.S.S., at Boston Navy Yard, mentioned, 44

Washington Navy Yard, refit of U.S.S. *Monitor*, 28; and photograph, 17; and photograph of five monitors, 69; and photograph, 85

Waite, Almira G., wife of A.P. Bashford, 41

Wassaw Sound: fight between the U.S.S. *Weehawken* (monitor) and the C.S.S. *Atlanta* (ironclad), 37

*Wassuc*, U.S.S. (monitor), mentioned, 58; and photograph at Charlestown Navy Yard, 59

Webb, William A., In command of C.S.S. *Atlanta* (ironclad), 65

*Weehawken*, U.S.S. (monitor), John Rodgers takes command, 36; and description of officer's quarters, 51; and mentioned, 58; and sinks while at anchor, 66

Weld, Francis, a surgeon aboard the U.S.S. *Nantucket* (monitor), 75

Wells, Gideon: accomplishments, 14; and appoints DuPont to the South Atlantic Blockading Squadron after Foote's death, 30; and assigns John Worden to dangerous secret mission, _; and comments on the light draft monitors, 60; and mentioned, 85

Williams, Barney, last Monitor survivor's claim, 44; and grave headstone photograph, 45

Woodbury, J.G., killed in action aboard U.S.S. *Catskill* (monitor), 34

Worden, John, untainted by treason, 24; and in Montgomery City jail, 24; and exchanged by Navy for Confederate naval officer, 25; and wounded in action aboard U.S.S. *Monitor*, 26; and photographed as Admiral, 27; and mentioned, 46; and his order to brace *Monitor's* crew with alcohol during pause in battle, 52; and letter addressed to him from his crew, 92

*Yazoo* class: failure of same, 58-59

# ABOUT THE AUTHOR

Jerry Harlowe is a native Virginian who comes from a long family tradition of military service. He proudly includes in his forefathers, five direct ancestors who served in the Army of Northern Virginia, two making the ultimate sacrifice and two others who were wounded.

Jerry moved to Maryland at age five and still resides there. He completed high school in 1965 and a year later enlisted in the United States Air Force. His duty stations included postings in Texas, Michigan and Virginia, but most importantly of all, Pleiku, Vietnam. "My life changed during my two tours. It was a change for the better and I still feel there has been no event in my life as powerful and altering. I'm glad I was there." Jerry plans to return to Vietnam in 2001, to "see the place without ducking" as he puts it.

Upon return to civilian life in July 1970, Jerry went to work for the Social Security Administration in Baltimore, Md. and continued his formal and informal education. He soon married Patricia, "his love at first sight," and they have raised two daughters and are now the proud grandparents of two.

Jerry's interest in the Civil War has been life long. He states, "As early as I can remember there was always talk of "THE WAR," which I came to understand at an early age was a part of my past and a part of my present." His interest in the navy, especially the monitors, came at the elementary school level when he read the book *Tin Can On A Shingle*.

He started writing about history in the 1970s, while a Civil War reenactor, for several journals, and has expanded to published articles in standard Civil War and naval magazines. In addition to this work on the monitor class ships of the Civil War, Jerry has authored and published a book on a soldier from Maryland in World War I, *Your Brother Will. The Letters and Diary of William Schellberg, 313th Machine Gun Company*. Jerry has written another book on the Battle of Monocacy and completed work on a Civil War history of Relay, Md., yet unpublished, and is currently working on a book that will be a photographic presentation of the U.S. sailors in the Asiatic Squadron, 1860-1917.

"I like reading and telling stories from the perspective of the individual" states Jerry. "In the vast sweep of time, of the glories and honors bestowed upon leaders, and the suffering of all, I can express better what I want to say in a context that I personally understand; one guy lost in the muck and mire of it all."

THOMAS PUBLICATIONS publishes books about the American Colonial era, the Revolutionary War, the Civil War, and other important topics. For a complete list of titles, visit our web site at:

http://thomaspublications.com

Or write to:

THOMAS PUBLICATIONS
P.O. Box 3031
Gettysburg, PA 17325